Wrestling with God

Wrestling with God

DEVOTIONAL READINGS FOR MEN

Introduction by
J. Lorne Peachey and Gordon Houser

Devotional readings and articles by
Ron Adams, Leonard Beechy, Matt Hamsher,
Gordon Houser, Allan Rudy-Froese, Doug Schulz,
Ervin Stutzman, and Philip Wiebe

Faith & Life Resources
A division of Mennonite Publishing Network
Mennonite Church USA and
Mennonite Church Canada

Scottdale, Pennsylvania
Waterloo, Ontario

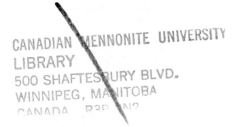

Library of Congress Cataloging-in-Publication Data
Wrestling with God : devotional readings for men / introduction by J. Lorne
Peachey and Gordon Houser.
    p. cm.
  ISBN 978-0-8361-9379-4 (pbk. : alk. paper)
  1. Christian men--Prayers and devotions. I. Peachey, J. Lorne, 1939- II.
Houser, Gordon.
  BV4843.W74 2007
  242'.642--dc22

                      2007017644

Wrestling with God: Devotional Readings for Men
Copyright © 2007 by Faith & Life Resources, a division of Mennonite Publishing
Network, Scottdale, PA 15683 and Waterloo, ON N2L 6H7

Unless otherwise noted, Scripture text is quoted, with permission, from the New
Revised Standard Version, © 1989, Division of Christian Education of the National
Council of Churches of Christ in the United States of America.

The publication of this book was made possible through funding from Mennonite
Men, a binational organization of Mennonite Church Canada and Mennonite
Church USA.

International Standard Book Number: 978-0-8361-9379-4
Cover and book design by Merrill R. Miller
Printed in USA

12 11 10 09 08 07   6 5 4 3 2 1

Orders and information:
USA: 800-245-7894
Canada: 800-631-6535
www.mph.org

TABLE OF CONTENTS

Introduction

All Christian men in our culture are called to respond to a number of issues that need to be addressed from their perspective as males. These include competition, sex, money, family, communication, leadership, and the roles of father, son, or brother. A particular challenge for many is to live as peacemakers in a world that challenges us to fight back.

How do we follow the way of Jesus, who is our supreme example of how to live faithfully as a man? How do we relate to God? How do we pass on God's blessing to a new generation, and especially to our sons? This book, offered by a group of Mennonite men, seeks to support men in doing all of these things.

A popular misconception of spirituality focuses almost exclusively on being happy or content as an individual. The writers of *Wrestling with God* assume that our spirituality involves much more than that. Spirituality means discipleship (learning to be a follower of Jesus), community (tangible, faithful fellowship with God's people), peace (living in right relationship with people and creation), and God's grace (acknowledging that we depend on God for our very being).

A masculine spirituality, writes Richard Rohr, will emphasize "movement over stillness, action over theory, service to the world over religious discussions, speaking the truth over social niceties, and doing justice instead of any self-serving 'charity.'"

Historically, Mennonite men have been fairly active in Christian service and promotion of justice. Generally, however, they have been less faithful in the practices of prayer, talking with one another, and sharing one another's woundedness.

These are some of the reasons why this book has come into being. More and more, men are looking for ways to cultivate their prayer lives as men, as they seek to live out their faith in today's world.

The way we have chosen to address spiritual needs of men is to look at some of the men in Scripture. These men provide both positive and negative examples of faithfulness and holiness. What do we learn from Jacob's wrestling with God and receiving a wound? What about Moses' leadership? David's adultery and anguish over his son Absalom? Joseph's role as husband to Mary? Peter's denial of Jesus and later his courageous act of welcoming Gentiles? Paul's confrontation of Peter and his encouragement to Timothy?

There are many rich examples from Scripture, and these devotionals and articles bring them alive for us. The articles include personal stories of the authors in their own pursuit of a mature Christian spirituality. The devotional readings, each only a page in length, include suggestions for reflection, discussion, or activity.

We pray that these meditations may serve to help men grow in wisdom and live more faithfully as servants of God.

Gordon Houser
J. Lorne Peachey

HOW TO USE THIS BOOK

Personal devotional times. Whether or not you have a regular routine of Bible reading and prayer, you can use these devotional reflections for personal times with God.

Men's gatherings. Sometimes it's difficult to find something appropriate for the opening of a meeting. These readings can spark some ideas.

Discussion groups. The articles or the devotional meditations can be springboards for discussion and sharing among men. To get the ball rolling, each meditation has two questions.

Articles on the Spiritual Growth of Men

1

Wrestling with God— Blessings in the wounds

BY GORDON HOUSER

My opponent, who outweighed me by 15 pounds, pressed my face against the blue mat. The smell of sweat and plastic filled my nostrils. My muscles ached, burning with lactic acid. My arms trembled with fatigue as I tried to lift myself. My opponent slipped his arm under mine and sought my neck in a half nelson. I had only to stay off my back to keep the match tied.

I'm at my limits, I thought. Yet I somehow mustered enough strength and willpower to force down his arm with mine and stay on my stomach. Finally, the whistle blew, and the match ended in a draw. I hardly had energy to get up and shake his hand.

In winter 1967-68, as a ninth grader at Lowther Junior High in Emporia, Kansas, I wrestled four matches against boys from other schools. I dreaded each match and wished I could somehow avoid it. I knew what lay ahead: six minutes of all-out effort that would tax all my physical and mental energy.

In my final match I could have won by forfeit because my opponent did not make weight (and I wrestled in a weight class higher than what I weighed, thus a 15-pound difference), but my coach said, "Let them wrestle."

I was able to avoid defeat that season largely because my older brothers had wrestled and taught me moves my opponents did not know. I also had some luck and refused to quit.

The story of Jacob wrestling "a man" he later says is God (Genesis 32:22-32) is full of meaning for men today. In this story, Jacob is at a crossroads. He has sent all his possessions across the Jabbok River (a play on his name). Now he is preoccupied with resolving the conflict with his brother, Esau, whose blessing he stole many years earlier.

Jacob is "left alone" (v. 24). Unlike many other sports, in wrestling you are alone on the mat with your opponent. Hearing the crowd around you telling you to get up when you don't feel an ounce of energy left in your body is a lonely, helpless feeling.

Although he has no crowd around him, Jacob feels some urgency to hold on to the man. He refuses to quit. The man even wounds Jacob on the hip—a rather cheap shot, it seems—but Jacob holds on and demands that the man bless him. The man does bless him, and then gives him a new name, Israel, which means "the one who strives with God."

Men tend to be more comfortable relating to the world physically. And while we understand striving to our limits in sports or work, we usually like to be in control. At least we like to win. But to strive with God, as Jacob's new name implies, leaves us out of control, unable to win, and wounded.

acob's wound reminds him of his call: to strive with God. His wound keeps him in a relationship with God.

Jacob's wound reminds him of his call: to strive with God. Jacob knows that from the womb he has always been a wrestler—and not always a fair one. He used deceit to gain advantage over others and often won, even though it harmed his relationships. In this story he is overmatched and receives a wound he carries the rest of his life, but this wound also keeps him in a relationship with God.

We men have trouble acknowledging our wounds, especially what some call the "father wound," the psychological hurt from an absent father. Richard Rohr writes that this can lead to "a life often with the passivity of an unlit fire." Remember that Jacob had been the favorite of his mother but not his father, who preferred Esau.

Men who don't grieve their pain and learn to transform it often transmit it in various ways: addictions, materialism, violence, and other ego-driven activities. Look at Jacob's life before his wrestling match. Women, on the other hand, tend to understand grief better because of their natural experience of loss through menstruating, gestating, and giving birth, not to mention the oppression that many encounter in our society.

When we consider engaging a God who will wound us, we may want to run. It takes courage, a certain strength, and a solid faith in God's love to hang in there and hold on until God blesses us.

After my ninth-grade year I had dreams of wrestling in high school and vying for a state championship. Instead I received a wound that became a blessing. My back had bothered me since a heavier teammate had hurt me in practice. I saw the doctor for my required physical that summer, and he discovered I had a growth deficiency in my lower vertebrae that prevented me from wrestling again.

My dream was shattered, but the following spring I had a spiritual experience in which I gave my life to Jesus Christ. Since then I've had other wounds and other spiritual experiences. None of them has been easy, yet each has drawn me closer to God's face.

Look at Jacob after his encounter with God. He limps to meet his brother, Esau, whom he fears will kill him, and they embrace. Jacob becomes Israel, the name for a people called to strive with God.

We, too, are called to strive to our limits and seek God's face, to look beyond the illusive images of God as judge or joker, warrior or weakling, and find that unconditional love we long for. As we wrestle with this God we find it so hard to believe in, as we acknowledge and grieve the wounds that leave us feeling bereft, we will find a healing in our lives that will allow us to help others experience a similar healing.

2

Plowing Emotional Ground

BY RON ADAMS

When I graduated from seminary in 1985, I knew I did not want to be a pastor. I had enjoyed my fellow students and the faculty. I loved every day of seminary. But I knew I would not be a pastor, at least right away.

There were many reasons for my decision. I was allergic to congregational politics. I was in transition between denominational affiliations, moving from Pentecostalism to Anabaptism. But today I know that it was mainly because I first had some work to do in my emotional life.

I grew up in a dysfunctional Christian home. My father was a pastor of a series of small congregations. During my growing-up years, I was in church whenever the doors were open. I lived and breathed the stories of Jesus and the testimonies of saints, whose lives were changed by his saving power. I heard my dad preach every Sunday, and my mom sing along to his guitar playing at Wednesday evening prayer meetings.

Home was an entirely different world. My parents' marriage was not well early on, and grew increasingly messy over the years. My father bitterly resented his treatment by uncaring parishioners. My mother suffered from depression and regularly withdrew from us. My siblings and I suffered my parents' anger, their violence, their disappointment. We were relieved when they finally separated.

I became an independent young adult, fell in love and married, and then felt called to seminary, even though I would not be ready for the pastorate. Then, a few years after seminary graduation, I experienced an emotional crisis that led me to seek counseling.

For two years, I met with my counselor and we walked together through the past. I came to understand my parents and myself in ways that were deep and ultimately life-changing. I realized that the dysfunction of my parents had helped shape both my mental health and my spirituality. Living in a home in which Christian piety went side by side with emotional violence had left me spiritually confused.

At the center of that confusion was my concept of God. As I struggled to hold together the God I heard described on Sunday and the God who seemed absent every other day, I eventually understood God to be random and unpredictable. God was to be approached carefully, since God's displeasure was to be feared. I knew I was supposed to love this God, and I understood intellectually that God loved me. But the relationship was one of mistrust. What I did for God I did from guilt and fear.

In short, my God looked and acted much like my parents. My relationship with them influenced my relationship with God. What was unhealthy in one became unhealthy in the other.

Slowly, with the help of my counselor, I reconstructed my understandings of myself and of God. Though that work is still in progress, I am in a far better place than before. I have learned to let go of the baggage given to me by my parents, or at least store it away where it cannot hurt me anymore. I have learned to love and worship God from a

have learned to love and worship God from a place of emotional healing, and to put away those images of God that do not bring life.

place of emotional healing, and to put away those images of God that do not bring life. I now see God most clearly in the loving, gentle, prophetic, and trustworthy Jesus of Nazareth.

This kind of soul work is not easy, especially for men. Many of us hang on to traditional ideas of manhood that make admitting needs difficult. Adding to the difficulty is the social stigma around mental health struggles. Yet if my experience is at all typical, I believe it is essential for us to lay down our defenses and engage in a process of healing of our wounded emotions and the distorted spirituality that comes from them.

Years after seeking help through counseling, I was invited to serve as interim pastor of my home congregation. I agreed to serve without hesitation. It felt to me then, and still does today, that the Holy Spirit was finally telling me to go ahead. I was ready.

I still had a lot to learn, but I had done the necessary work of getting my emotional house in order. Or to be more truthful, I had at least tidied things up enough to live there more comfortably.

In his parable of the sower (Matthew 13:1-9), Jesus describes what happens when his word falls on various types of soil. When it falls on well-tended, well-prepared ground, it flourishes. Likewise, in doing the work of emotional healing, we create a better place for that word to flourish within us. In finding emotional healing, our spirits too are healed, and we can truly love, enjoy, and worship God.

3

Time, Tennis, and Things Worth Keeping

BY LEONARD BEECHY

I was sitting with my mom at her table in the nursing home, helping her eat her lunch. Seated to our right was Helen, aged 102. Helen was having one of her silent days, I thought. But as I reached for Mom's water glass, Helen suddenly fixed me with a stare. "What time is it?" she demanded. I told her it was twenty minutes until noon. Her eyes left me to face forward again. "Tempus fugit," she said.

Tempus fugit. Time flies. Literally, the Latin expression means, "Time flees." She may have been speaking of her morning or of her life. Either way, I knew what she meant, and I'm only a little over half her age.

Earlier that week I had been to the doctor. The pain had begun around Christmas, a dull, sullen ache creeping like doubt from my lower back and down my right leg. My Internet sources pointed to sciatica, probably from a bulging lumbar disc. After watching me wince through several contortions, my doctor thought so too. To confirm the source, we'd have to do an expensive MRI. Instead, we agreed that I'd try physical therapy.

Sciatica for a man my age is about as common as hair loss. So why was I so despondent? It seemed unfair, that's why. I'm a fanatic about health and fitness: Workouts with weights and running at least three times a week, disciplined eating to stay lean—all for one of the loves of my life: tennis.

I love everything about tennis—the sounds, the physical challenge, the equipment, the competition, the harmonious movement. Every week before the pain started, year-round, I played at least one singles and one doubles match. Just before Christmas I had won the singles league at my club. Now I couldn't walk without limping, couldn't get into the car without groaning, couldn't put on my right sock without help from my wife. What kind of reward was this for all my careful discipline and training?

At bottom, this became a spiritual question. I believe in salvation as shalom: a state of spiritual, physical, and emotional wholeness. Jesus healed, not just to authenticate his divine mission, but also to actually bring salvation. "Your faith has saved you," he tells the blind man of Jericho (Luke 18:42), to give only one of many examples in the Gospels. Jesus' ministry of salvation sometimes meant physical healing, sometimes exorcising a demon, sometimes forgiving sins, sometimes—as in the case of Zacchaeus—straightening out bad financial practices. To be saved is to be released from whatever makes you less than whole in every part of your being.

The problem is that as I age—and as my friends, my mother, and my colleagues age—I am more and more confronted not with wholeness but with impairment. Yes, I know: My bout with sciatica is a tiny problem compared to the chronic, debilitating, and progressive physical illnesses we can all count among just our friends, family, and congregation. But I'm also becoming more aware of the emotional and mental impairment that afflicts people close to me: depression, bipolar disorder, addiction. My daughter works with men who live with moderate developmental disabilities. Intellectually, verbally, socially, they will always live within these limitations.

Limitations. Just saying the word pushes us toward a troubling observation: Impairment is normal. As we age, impairment is not just possible; it's inevitable. This does not make any particular impairment easier, nor does it make them all equally hellish. Each is unique. But as we begin to look at impairment as a normal human experience, what can we say about its spiritual dimensions?

Paul the apostle knew about impairment firsthand. Scholars can reach no conclusions about what his "thorn in the flesh" really was: A problem with his eyes? A psychological disorder? What we do know is that it troubled Paul so much that he prayed three times to have it removed, and three times God refused him. Talk about unfair! Here is the man charged with establishing the Christian gospel in the world. Paul knows that he could fulfill this mission much more easily without this "thorn in the flesh," and yet God refuses to remove it. And why? Because, God says to Paul, "Power is made perfect in weakness" (2 Corinthians 12:9).

What? Is God telling Paul that there is something in human impairment that completes the power of God? Certainly this belongs among the great paradoxes—and great truths—of our upside-down faith. Our experience of impairment can keep us aware of God's grace and power.

Nothing in Paul's conversation with God about his "thorn in the flesh" offers us an adequate answer to the problem of human suffering. For that, we may do better to look in the direction of the cross. But still— don't we find that when we are reminded of our mortality, when we experience the pain and limitation of earthly life, are we not also given a stronger sense of that which is eternal, that which "abides"?

My sciatic pain responded well to physical therapy. I recently won a small local tennis tournament. Little pulses of pain, however, remind me that this is likely a chronic condition, like Jacob's limp after his own wrestling with God (Genesis 32). The pain also reminds me of God's faithfulness through it all.

Others around me are teaching me what it means to let impairment point us to God. Some from my congregation who experience depression, for example, have begun meeting regularly to ensure that no one will have to walk this dark journey alone or in silence.

When I last visited my mother, she didn't know where she was or why. But she did begin singing a hymn, and I joined her for all four verses, each ending with this refrain from the words of Paul:

> But I know whom I have believed
> And am persuaded that he is able
> To keep that which I've committed
> Unto him against that day. (Daniel H. Whittle)

Helen, 102 years old, recently told me, "Some days it seems so useless to be alive. Then someone shows they care about me, and I feel like it's worth living another day."

So Helen, in her wheelchair at the table, lives another day. *Tempus fugit*. But a moment of caring has an eternal air about it. Time flies. Our bodies and minds fail. But God's grace is sufficient, and faith, hope, and love abide.

4

Tussling with God in the Day's Details

BY DOUG SCHULZ

"You have striven with God and with humans, and have prevailed."
(Jacob's Challenger, Genesis 32:28)

Wrestling is the perfect term for how we engage life's decisions and directions. Can I get through even one day without grappling with problems—my own or someone else's? For example, I had set aside today to write about the spiritual life as a lock-arm tussle between my ego and God's will—but I ended up having to take on a list of other challenges.

Breakfast done, I had just finished writing the first sentence when my 22-year-old son came in. I mentioned my writing project. We reminisced—about play fights on the basement rug when he was little; arm-wrestles when he was a weight-lifting teenager; and a recent friendly tangle where he pushed this fifty-something father out of the kitchen. Then we tackled his career; a job demand is raising implications for his wedding date, living location, and his fiancée's educational plans. I countered his anxiety by claiming God's concern when things become complicated. He appreciated that.

We wrestled over his issues, but since I was his father, they also became mine. It was nice to be needed, but it takes a heap of energy.

My son left, and the phone rang—a former colleague from across the country. Half a year ago she lost her closest spiritual sister to a rare disease. Today she floundered in a dark stage of grief. I listened, gave encouragement, promised prayer. An important conversation, but exhausting.

After that, lunchtime. My wife and I chatted over the vegetable soup we'd eaten all week while we're waging that war called "wrestling with weight." We discussed the challenges we carry as we support our children and friends. This led to memories of a struggle years earlier, when work stress strained our relationship almost too far. The meal lasted longer than usual. We worked through feelings, reminding each other of our mutual effort and God's guidance, which kept us best friends now.

The rest of the day kept my writing project at bay. A debate with my other son over gas money for the car. Several hours of headaches as I marked a stack of papers for my high school English students, encountering grammatical mistakes, lack of creativity, and plagiarism. A quick trip to the service station for an oil change and some quibbling over the amount charged for a recent repair. A battle at suppertime with my gag reflex over another beloved bowl of soup. The mortal realization that I had writing to do, leaving no time for *Hockey Night in Canada* on television.

The point of this litany is that my life is a series of wrestling matches. I was born to be a wrestler day after day. That role won't discourage me if, like Jacob, I recognize that God is intimately involved in my life. I can always grow to appreciate better how God fits into the skirmishes and scuffles of day-to-day living. I can grow in my understanding of how God influences the grand scheme of my life, building it up, and directing it forward. I'm not fighting alone or for nothing.

 was born to be a wrestler day after day. That role won't discourage me if, like Jacob, I recognize that God is intimately involved in my life.

There's no spiritual satisfaction in many of the things that men tend to brag about, like counting up scalps taken through victorious arguments with loved ones, friends, or enemies. Or recounting hero stories about those tough times we've survived by grit 'n' grimace and a dash or more of grace. Or claiming fame as a victim, overpowered or sidelined by the wrongful moves of others.

The story of Jacob's wrestle with God teaches that the spiritual life of a healthy man is grounded in an honest admission: that true connection with God and others is about relationships where we take seriously the face, more than the force, of God and others. As spiritual people we wrestle not to win, but to be with. We deal with life's difficulties in order to care about people more, not less. We aim to serve them better, not just to prevent them from disturbing us.

If we want to know God richly, we have to let God bless us through our struggles, as Jacob did. That way, though the pains from wrestling may go with us, the power of the blessing guides us in doing God's will, enjoying God's favor, in all of life's journeys.

"Just to be is blessing," writes Abraham Heschel. "Just to live is holy." Let's admit to be alive is to be a wrestler. So, each day's holy blessing is in wrestling . . . *with* God.

5

A Sort-of Guide to Almost-Devotions

BY PHILIP WIEBE

The best thing I've ever learned about doing daily devo-tions is that there's no biblical command saying, "Thou shalt do daily devotions." What a relief. Oops, did I say that out loud? Let me explain.

I grew up in a churchgoing household that followed a firm set of spir-itual routines. We attended church every Sunday morning and evening, and every Wednesday night. We contributed to the church offer-ing every week. We prayed before every meal. We read devotions before each dinnertime. Many years of this convinced me that good Christians did certain God Things at clockwork intervals.

I know the intent of my family's pursuit of Christian duty was not to make faith seem like a dry checklist of weekly spiritual chores. Yet by the time I finished grade school, that was how it felt. We always did devotions before dinner, I figured, to keep God happy. I, on the other hand, was not happy as I sneaked peeks at the waiting food while the reading of the meditation went on and on.

Today I'm aware of many Christian men who are stuck in the "devo-tions as duty" syndrome. In small groups and other settings, I've encour-aged guys to develop regular devotional times for reflecting on Scripture, praying, and seeking God's presence. The most common reaction has been, "I know I should do that, but . . . " There's too much work to do, reading the Bible is challenging, life is always hectic, and so on. It's hard to start doing devotions.

But I don't say, "You need to do it anyway" or "Here, let me give you a nice daily devotional guide." The first thing I try to encourage is a change of perspective.

For me this began to happen when I entered my teens. Around that time we moved to Southern California, where my father became pastor of a newly planted church. The atmosphere here was different from anything I'd experienced before. There were many new Christians in the congregation, and strong influences came from that era's burgeoning Jesus Movement.

Over the next several years I learned that "doing devotions" was less about "doing" and more about "devotion." It involved the desire to develop a personal relationship with God, not a wish to placate God by doing spiritual homework. As I look back on that change of heart, three events stand out.

First, our growing church hired a youth pastor who demonstrated a joyful passion about knowing God and studying the Bible. My past experience had made these seem kind of mundane. It amazed me now to see a young adult so obviously excited about following Jesus and growing in the faith. That was something I wanted to try.

Second, our youth group went on a weekend retreat that had a special impact on me. It didn't seem so promising at first. We were heading out into the Mojave Desert for a prayer retreat. *Wonderful,* I thought in my teenage cynicism. But once we were there, camping

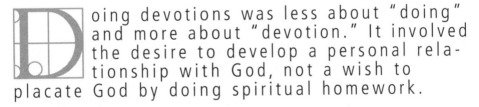

Doing devotions was less about "doing" and more about "devotion." It involved the desire to develop a personal relationship with God, not a wish to placate God by doing spiritual homework.

in the Joshua Tree National Monument with a simple agenda of reading our Bibles, praying, writing in journals, and talking about our insights and experiences, I became transfixed. The otherworldly landscape, the quest for God's presence, the extended reflection on the Word—these completely enraptured me. So this was what *real* devotional endeavors were like.

Third, as a young man of 20, I ventured into the countryside as part of a touring music ministry. This would be fun, playing lots of guitar and performing for multitudes of adoring fans. Or so I thought. In reality, I quickly encountered the many challenges of trying to work effectively and live in harmony with my bandmates. This created in me an urgency to spend time in prayer and seek wisdom from the Bible.

Sometime later I realized that Jesus' pattern of work and retreat didn't follow a sensible time management plan. He didn't consult his day planner every morning, with the devotional half-hour penciled in at 6 or 7 a.m. Jesus involved himself in intensive periods of work for days on end, followed by complete removal from the scene for extended times of spiritual renewal. This approach probably wouldn't work for most of us now, but it does teach us a few things:

1. **No special holiness is granted to those who do devotions the same time, the same place, seven days a week.** That may work well for some people, but not for everyone. There are all kinds of ways to make time for God. Applying some creativity in this area, based on each of our unique personalities and life-schedules, is a good thing.

2. **It all starts with the relationship.** Years of required dinnertime devotions did little to develop my relationship with God. But later, a little desire to get to know God did wonders for developing my devotional life. Simply wanting to know God is always the best motivation for praying, reading the Bible, and seeking God's touch in our lives.

3. **It helps to get real about our need for God.** We men tend to focus heavily on getting the work done and pressing on no matter what, even when we really want to fall down and cry, "Lord, help me!" Developing a consistent devotional life is more about saying "Lord, help me!" than stoically doing devotions because we perceive it's the required task.

Now, after all of this, if you want to get started on your daily devotional plan, then go for it. If you'd rather try for longer periods of contemplation every other day or so, that's good too. If you want to go out in the desert for a weekend of reflection and journaling, then let me know, because I'm right there with you.

Devotional
Readings

1. KEEPING TRACK OF MY BROTHER

[Cain said,] "Am I my brother's keeper?"—Genesis 4:9

Scripture: Genesis 4:4b-12

It is sobering that the first Bible story about brothers is an account of competition, jealously, deceit, and murder. Cain, tiller of land, was so angry with his shepherd brother Abel that he lured him onto his own turf and killed him.

Here the text flags murder as the most heinous way of dealing with the conflict that is always present in close relationships. When God asks Cain where his brother is, Cain responds, "Am I my brother's keeper?" or, as the New Living Translation has it: "Am I supposed to keep track of him?" (v. 9).

On Cain's lips is the solution to the problem. Yes, he is supposed to be keeping track of his brother even though they have experienced conflict.

The last part of the book of Genesis shows a positive view of what "keeping track" of one's brother might look like. Joseph, even after his brothers have sold him into slavery, takes the initiative to reconcile with his brothers (Genesis 42-45). Even though pride, conflict, and deceit have been a part of the past, the resolution is found in love, in brothers who are willing to "keep track" of each other.

If you are a normal sibling, friend, or spouse, you will have conflict in your relationships. But rather than seeking to harm the other, this story says you can seek understanding and reconciliation and "keep track" of each other in love.

—Allan Rudy-Froese

Thank you, God, for the close relationships that I have. In spite of the disagreements I am bound to have, help me to always "keep track" of them in love.

When did you last have an argument with a close friend or loved one? How do you care for people even in the midst of disagreements?

2. GOD WORKS—EVEN WHEN WE FAIL

[Abraham said,] "Say you are my sister, so that it may go well with me because of you, and that my life may be spared on your account."
—Genesis 12:13

Scripture: Genesis 12:10-20

Sometimes men, who think of themselves as protectors, instead put women at risk to save their own skin. That is the case with Abram, who asks Sarai to pass on a half-truth about their relationship as they enter Egypt. (According to Genesis 20:12, Sarai was Abram's half-sister.) Sarai is beautiful, so Abram fears that Pharaoh's servants will kill him in order to get his wife.

Abram's action is difficult for me to defend. I am shocked that with the first words this father of the Hebrew people speaks in the Bible, he intends to deceive. Even worse, nowhere does Scripture say directly that Abram is wrong for perpetrating this deception. We have no word of repentance or regret from Abram. Instead, he gains wealth by his actions.

It is the Egyptian king who suffers because of Abram's deception. When the Lord inflicts diseases on Pharaoh's household, Pharaoh rebukes Abram for his deception. Then Pharaoh's servants escort Abram and his entourage out of town.

How can this story build our faith as Christians? Perhaps its chief value is to show what can happen when a man takes things into his own hands and tries to accomplish goals with lies and deceit. The same powerful God who later gives Abram and Sarai a promised son could well have protected them from Pharaoh's lustful gaze without Abram's half-truth. Yet in the face of Abram's faults and lack of faith, God stands by him. As we see from the rest of the story, God works out divine purposes, despite our human failings.

—Ervin Stutzman

Thank you, God, for your redeeming grace, which saves us in spite of our failures.

What is God doing in and behind this story? What does the story tell us about our need for protection and control?

3. GOD IN UNLIKELY PLACES

King Melchizedek of Salem brought out bread and wine; he was a priest of God Most High. He blessed him and said, "Blessed be Abram."
—Genesis 14:18-19

Scripture: Genesis 14:17-24; Hebrews 7

As an outdoorsy 19-year-old, I read a book by the naturalist Edward Abbey about his seasons as a park ranger in the stark Southwest canyon lands. His interaction with the landscape inspired me to look for more of God's creative presence in nature.

I liked Abbey's book so much that I recommended it to a friend. A week later he came back with a sour face and plenty of criticism. It didn't sit well with my friend that the author was known as a rogue and rebel rather than an upstanding churchgoer. Still, that didn't change my belief that God had spoken to me through this unconventional source.

Something similar happens when Melchizedek, King of Salem and a priest of God, blesses Abraham. On reading the Genesis account, one might think, *where did that guy come from?* Melchizedek has not been mentioned before and does not appear again in Genesis. He is called "a priest of God" before God ever appoints a priestly line. Can we trust Melchizedek's credentials?

The author of Hebrews says yes. Melchizedek is appointed "not through a legal requirement" but by the power of God (7:16). He is a picture of Jesus, our permanent high priest, who "always lives to make intercession for" us (7:25; see Psalm 110:4).

As with Edward Abbey and Melchizedek, God can inspire and guide in unexpected ways, even outside "authorized" methods. Wherever my day or my life might take me, God is able to bless me and speak to me however God chooses.

—Philip Wiebe

God, you can get through to me wherever I am. I need that in my world, where many don't believe in you or follow your ways. I'm looking for your unexpected blessings.

How open are you to receiving God's guidance and inspiration from unusual sources? Are you willing to follow God's ways even when that isn't the popular choice?

4. "HERE I AM"

After these things God tested Abraham. He said to him, "Abraham!" And he said, "Here I am."—Genesis 22:1

Scripture: Genesis 22:1-19

The mother of one of my teaching colleagues died last week. The next day I found out that a longtime friend and tennis partner had decided to end his troubled marriage. Both situations called for me to step up, to do something.

What can I really do to help? I wondered. But I also knew this was no time for hesitation: To be a friend or a colleague, to be a family member, to be a caring person—there is no choice. You have to make the phone call. You have to go. What do you say? The truth is, if love guides you, it doesn't matter. All you need to communicate is what you say by showing up: "Here I am."

In this troubling story, Abraham says it three times. The first time is just before God gives him instructions for the most painful job God ever gave a father. The second time he says it is to Isaac, his beloved son. Yes, Abraham is there for him too, even if the truth, as far as he knows it, is too terrible to speak. The third time is when the voice from heaven stops the knife in Abraham's hand. The story is silent about Abraham's inner life. But whether his heart is breaking with grief or overflowing with relief, Abraham is there, really there—for his God and for his son.

Some say that 80 percent of success is showing up. So is 99 percent of caring. Any cry of need is a call from God. The challenge is to answer even the most difficult call with three words: "Here I am."

—Leonard Beechy

Here I am, Lord. No matter what else seems important, today I will be present, really there, to you and to those I care about.

What parts of your life seem too important to really allow yourself to be available to God? What keeps you from being available to those who need you?

5. A FACE BEYOND RAGE

Esau said, "Let us journey on our way, and I will go alongside you."
—Genesis 33:12

Scripture: Genesis 27:41-45; Genesis 33

I wince when I realize that Jacob managed to wangle what really belonged to Esau. My own brothers were fair men, but I've been "done" once or twice by supposed Christians.

We've all likely been hurt one way or another by a brother. For men like Esau, rip-offs boil the blood. Red-faced, he snarls, "I will kill my brother!" (27:41). Wrath may feel righteous, but it almost always leads us to think, say, or do regrettable things.

How can we rework outrage and focus on forgiveness? In this brotherhood story, the time comes when the men must face one another again after many years apart. Fearing revenge, Jacob loads Esau with gifts (Genesis 32). Whether Jacob's gesture or something else soothes Esau's soul, when he meets the offender, Esau reaches out in peace (33:4).

Embraced, Jacob responds, "Truly, to see your face is like seeing the face of God" (v. 10). But immediately, though reconciled, Jacob apparently pulls another trick! Sidestepping Esau's offer of fellowship, he makes off to build prosperity on his own (vv. 12-17).

So, what is the moral here? Insofar as it depends on us, act rightly. Go toward the wrongdoer. Show the face of God in front of our brother, whether he turns toward us or not. Jacob, though spiritual, was sometimes a swindler, a soul who could weasel a brother.

Sometimes we will meet this breed of man. When we do, will he see the face of God in us?

—Doug Schulz

Lord, I have to admit that I have not always been the brother I should be. Thank you for your forgiveness. Help me think of that when someone offends me.

Silently name or visualize a person who has hurt you. Think also of a person you have somehow victimized. What clear guidance is God giving to you about those situations?

6. FACE TO FACE

Jacob called the place Peniel, saying, "I have seen God face to face, and yet my life is preserved."—Genesis 32:30

Scripture: Genesis 32:22-32

Imagine the shock of spending the night wrestling someone, then discovering you have just wrestled God. Like Jacob, you likely walk away (or limp away) changed.

Jacob is in a fearful state. He is about to meet his brother, Esau, whom he has cheated out of his inheritance. To protect his family and possessions, he sends them across the Jabbok (perhaps a play on Jacob's name) River, while he stays behind, alone (vv. 22-24).

Does anything drive us away from God's face (or presence) more than fear? Alone, Jacob wrestles a man "until daybreak." This sudden event leaves him no time to be afraid.

Relying on his instincts instead of conniving to avoid what he fears, Jacob holds on and demands that the man bless him. The man does bless him, and then gives him a new name, Israel, which means "the one who strives with God."

My most intense experiences of intimacy with God, of meeting God face to face, have usually come through striving—either with my conscience or with things not going my way. Facing our fears and striving with God can take us beyond our fears into a deeper experience of that mysterious Love that leaves us limping, marked as one who has wrestled God.

Jacob names the place where he has wrestled this figure "Peniel," which means the face of God. He is surprised to have survived. We, too, have the fearsome privilege of facing God, if we have the courage. And who knows how that may change us?

—Gordon Houser

Give me courage, Lord, to strive with you, to bring my desires and needs to you and seek your blessing.

When have you felt afraid and faced that fear? How did this change you?

7. HIDDEN OPPORTUNITIES

Moses said, "I must turn aside and look at this great sight, and see why the bush is not burned up."—Exodus 3:3

Scripture: Exodus 3:1-4:17

That day in the wilderness, Moses faces two critical challenges that still confront us today. The first is to "turn aside" from daily routine, for only then can Moses recognize the burning bush for what it truly is: holy ground.

It can be difficult for us as men to turn aside, relinquishing day-to-day responsibilities long enough to hear God calling us in what could be life-changing ways. Can we stop trying to get things done long enough to hear God calling us to deeper reorientations?

Moses' second challenge is to accept the task that God asks him to do. Here Moses is less of a positive example. He asks God, "Who am I?" (3:11). This response might not be so surprising if we remember that God is asking Moses to return to Egypt, a scene of past failure and betrayal. There his efforts to respond to the Israelites' suffering have ended in his fleeing to Midian.

In exile, Moses finds a wife, starts a family, and has a secure job as a shepherd for his father-in-law. Why risk it all to return to Egypt? Because God's call comes with reassurances as well as risks. God promises to be with Moses, to provide human companionship in his brother Aaron, and to do miracles to back up Moses' calling.

Responding to God's call can be a terrifying experience, especially if it involves setting aside our present securities or overcoming past failures, but God's promises prove greater than the risks.

—Matt Hamsher

From the burning bush in our own lives, let us hear your voice today, Lord. Help us to say not just "Here I am," but also "Send me."

What are you doing or could you do in your life to turn aside to hear God's call? What promises or reassurances do you need to hear from God?

8. TIME TO GIVE THANKS

The Lord is my strength and my might, and he has become my salvation.
—Exodus 15:2

Scripture: Exodus 15:1-20

For most of us, life presents a profusion of ups and downs, challenges and triumphs, glad times and sad times. For me, all of these have happened in the last two hours. To get through the daily grind, it helps to practice thankfulness. And it does take a lot of practice!

Though it's not easy to maintain, a grateful attitude helps us embrace the blessings and cope with the difficulties of life. I try to practice thankfulness with brief prayers and words of praise to God throughout the day.

But sometimes the challenge a person faces is much more than momentary. It could be an ongoing trial lasting months or years, from which there seems to be little hope of escape. This is the case for God's people enduring centuries of slavery in Egypt. How can anyone give thanks in such a situation?

Yet God finally provides a way out. Through the famous parting of the Red Sea, Moses leads the people to freedom. And though there will be many more trials to come, now it is time to give thanks. This is more than a brief prayer or quick word of praise. In this psalm, we have Moses' long and detailed song about God's strength and salvation, which the people greatly enjoy and sing with much expression and enthusiasm.

Brief praises and prayers are great, but often God deserves more. During my days I want to take time and care to offer heartfelt thanks to my Savior and Provider. That's the kind of worship God richly deserves.

—Philip Wiebe

Lord, during my busy days I won't forget that you are my strength, my might, and my salvation. I trust you to help me face life's difficulties.

Do you thank God enough for acts of deliverance and salvation, as well as for daily strength and provision? Where can you carve out time for worship and praise?

9. DON'T LOOK AWAY

[Moses entreated the Lord,] "Let me cross over to see the good land beyond the Jordan, that good hill country and the Lebanon."—Deuteronomy 3:25

Scripture: Deuteronomy 3:23-29

My dad left us just as I was graduating from college in 1978. Since then, he has visited rarely. It was a shock, therefore, when I found him standing outside my office door, asking to come in.

He sobbed as I embraced him. He told me of his life, whose steady theme is regret. He regrets leaving us behind and not coming back. He also mourns the accumulated consequences of other bad decisions and poor choices he has made. When he left my office with familiar words of promise to come again soon, I did my own weeping.

So much of who I am as a man is rooted in my opposition to what I'd seen my father do. Learning from his mistakes, I have lived a much happier, much less regretful life. It has not been a perfect life by any stretch, but I have been able to taste the fruit of better choices, and I have known the benefits of faithfulness.

Our text reminds us of the agony of regret. So close to the Promised Land, Moses can only look on it from a distance. His past failure prevents his coming any closer. One hopes that Moses finds some solace in knowing that what he cannot do, his people can do. Following Joshua, they will enter the Promised Land.

It's a stark scene before us. We are tempted to look away. Yet, there is a cautionary wisdom in such stories, wisdom that may make all the difference in our next hard choice.

—Ron Adams

Lord, help me to be true to what you want for me today. Keep me from actions I know I will later regret. Keep visions of your Promised Land before me.

What tough choices are in front of you today? Of the many possibilities, which response will draw you closer to the "promised land" God has in store for you?

10. MENTORING IN STRENGTH AND IN WEAKNESS

Joshua son of Nun was full of the spirit of wisdom because Moses had laid his hands on him.—Deuteronomy 34:9

Scripture: Deuteronomy 34:9 and Joshua 1:1-9

In his 70s my grandfather confessed to me that he smoked as a young man and still craved a cigarette once in a while. This revelation shocked me because my grandfather, Peter Froese, was a humble pillar of the Mennonite Church. For decades he had served as a pastor in British Columbia. His comment made me respect him all the more, for it shed light on his humanity and on how he dealt prayerfully with his struggles.

We tend to look at the strengths of mentors but do not always see the whole person—including their struggles. It would be easy to ponder the good things that Joshua has learned from Moses, such as strong faith, a can-do attitude, and obvious leadership skills. But Moses also has a past that includes murder, a tendency to run away from problems, and the pressing problem of anger toward God. The "wisdom" Moses passes on to Joshua has been gained as much from Moses' struggles and brokenness as from his winning qualities.

It is important that we be honest about our sins and struggles as we mentor others. In leaving a legacy with others, we do best to package it in vulnerability and thankfulness for God's grace, rather than in bravado about our talents and accomplishments.

—Allan Rudy-Froese

Thank you, God, for mentors. Help me to be an honest mentor, sharing my strengths and weaknesses so that others may see your amazing grace.

Questions: What are the strengths and weaknesses of the mentors in your life? What do you want younger men to say about you at your funeral?

11. AWED BY GOD'S POWER

When Gideon heard the telling of the dream and its interpretation, he worshiped. —Judges 7:15

Scripture: Judges 7:15-22

Last week at our church, an 88-year-old man told of a time 61 years ago when God spoke to him in a worship service. A few days after that experience, he received an invitation to serve with an organization that knew nothing of his spiritual encounter.

This dual confirmation brought clarity out of the man's vocational confusion and guided him for the next fifty years of his life's work. It was such a sacred moment that he hardly dared tell about it to his scholarly friends. Last week was the first time he shared this story in public.

The story of Gideon is an even more dramatic account of God's vocational leading. Gideon seeks God's confirmation by laying out a fleece (Judges 6:36-40). Twice while Gideon is mustering his army, God asks him to reduce his forces, leaving him only 300 men to face the vast Midianite army, "thick as locusts" in the valley (7:12). God doesn't want the Israelites to claim credit for themselves when the Midianite army is vanquished. Any victory in this battle will come only by God's miraculous action.

When Gideon is afraid again, God offers him another sign, the interpreted dream of a Midianite soldier. It is the encouragement that Gideon needs. He is so moved that he bows down and worships.

God does not leave us to our own devices in hard times. Rather, God invites us to receive his gracious deliverance by faith.

—Ervin Stutzman

Thank you, God, for your promised deliverance in the midst of seemingly impossible circumstances.

God does not always answer our prayers in the dramatic fashion told in the story of Gideon. Think of a time when God answered a prayer or intervened in your behalf, even in a small way.

12. WHAT A WEDDING!

Boaz said to the elders and all the people, "Today you are witnesses."
—*Ruth 4:9*

Scripture: Ruth 3:16; Ruth 4

I grew up with older half-siblings in the house. I watched some meet their life mates. Most found partners from our background. But I remember the day one sister brought a squirming "stranger" in for parental scrutiny. The man supplied an acceptable faith story, so my folks nodded approval. I ushered at the wedding.

In the time of Boaz and Ruth, huge spiritual, social, and economic obligations are attached to marriage. Personal inconvenience and possible embarrassment may meet a man who marries outside normal expectations. Relatives and friends can turn away. Men of influence avoid the wrong sort of woman.

Boaz is impressed by the qualities of loyalty and courage that the Moabite Ruth, a non-Hebrew, has showed. Risking reputation and resources, he proves himself to be loyal to Hebrew custom; he pledges to maintain Ruth's husband's name and property rights. Then, boldly honorable toward an outsider, Boaz declares to community leaders that he'll gladly take this woman in.

Bible scholars explain this wonderful story as the practice of "kinsmen redemption." Some say it's a picture of Christ's mission—paying a price to redeem us all from soul poverty, from namelessness before God, so we can be forever united with Christ.

The story is not just symbolic; it's also a mandate. We must use all means to aid the helpless, especially those marginalized, to ensure them a home and a name.

—Doug Schulz

Lord, I want to be a witness to your redemptive power bringing happiness to the homeless and outcast. To that end, show me my opportunity, and help me fulfill duty.

What opportunities is God giving me to help victims of a difficult life situation? What price may I need to pay to follow this call and make a real difference?

13. EYES GUIDED BY LOVE

David sent messengers to get [Bathsheba], and she came to him, and he lay with her.—2 Samuel 11:4

Scripture: 2 Samuel 11:1-5

God has created us men in such a way that we are sexually motivated through the eyes. When our eyes tell us that a woman is attractive, we consider the possibility of relationship. For many of us, what began as speechless wonder at a woman's physical beauty gradually led to a whole relationship in marriage. Here, we were free to explore the wonder of sexual love, open at last to the full beauty of our partner.

We also see the destructive turns that sexual attraction can take. When we permit lust to guide our choices, we begin to see women as objects for our use. We think their only purpose is to satisfy our sexual needs. Beyond that point lies a wasteland of suffering inflicted and received. In that wasteland lust rules, leaving little room for love.

One afternoon King David's eyes wander to a woman bathing. He desires her. He sends for her. His lust leads him to rape and murder. From that point can be traced all the sorrow he later endures. The pain he has caused Bathsheba will finally be mirrored in his own life, as David's fortunes dwindle and his children suffer.

Sexual attraction is a good thing, created by God. It is often the first step toward lasting love. But as we know too well, good gifts can be distorted. Like everything else in our lives, our eyes must be guided by the Spirit of Christ.

—Ron Adams

Lord, you created me to be drawn to what is beautiful. Help me to hold this gift under your rule of love. Keep my vision pure this day.

Questions: How difficult is it for you to have love guide your eyes? Where might you turn today for help in meeting that goal?

14. COVERING UP

[David wrote,] "Set Uriah in the forefront of the hardest fighting, and then draw back from him, so that he may be struck down and die."
—2 Samuel 11:15

Scripture: 2 Samuel 11:14-27

Have you ever watched someone try to cover one wrong deed with another, only to find that things began falling apart? At times we see such scenarios played out on the evening news. As revealed in its 2001 bankruptcy, the giant energy firm Enron was caught in such a spiral. Sadly, even self-professed Christians were convicted at the top levels in that accounting scandal.

King David learns the hard way that one sin can lead to another until events spin out of control. David tries his best to get Uriah to sleep with his wife, to cover up David's sin of adultery. But Uriah refuses to cooperate, choosing to demonstrate his loyalty to the king.

In a deeply ironic twist, this Hittite foreigner shows himself so loyal to the king of Judah—and, in fact, to the requirements of religious law—that the king's cover-up doesn't work. So David sends word to the battlefront by Uriah's own hand, assuring that he will be killed in battle. Uriah likely goes to his grave without knowing that David had conspired to steal both his wife and his life.

This story shows that wrong choices can quickly multiply when one is trying to cover up a wrong deed. When we find ourselves going down the wrong path, the best thing to do is to make the U-turn called repentance. God honors those who step out of the darkness and into the light.

—Ervin Stutzman

God, help me to open my heart to you and others. Forgive me for the times when I have tried to cover up my wrongs.

If David had been able to foresee the consequences of his sin, how might he have acted differently? When have you seen one wrong lead to another in a cover-up attempt? What were the consequences?

15. TRUE CONFESSIONS

David said to Nathan, "I have sinned against the Lord."
—2 Samuel 12:13

Scripture: 2 Samuel 12:1-20

When a public figure is caught in some wrongdoing, it can be fascinating to hear the person's reaction. I heard two good ones recently from a couple of different celebrities. Upon arrest for a federal crime, one said "They're trying to make an example of me." Another, after causing a nightclub riot, did offer an apology but quickly added, "Some other people started it."

Such responses are common these days. People who do wrong try to pass the blame or apologize in a way that sounds less than sincere.

The sins that King David commits are far worse than the usual celebrity's lapse of judgment. If a leader today gets involved in such a tangle of adultery and murder, it generates sensational headlines for months. Yet when the prophet Nathan confronts David, the king shows no hesitation, no passing of blame, no drumming up of excuses. David simply says, "I have sinned against the Lord." He takes full responsibility and earnestly seeks God's forgiveness, even though he will have to live with the difficult consequences of his actions.

It's unlikely that any of us will ever do a wrong that makes national headlines. When we do mess up, however, let us fight the temptation to hide the truth, pass the blame, or flee the consequences. It is only through sincere confession before God and those we've hurt that we can we find true forgiveness and freedom.

—Philip Wiebe

Lord, have mercy on me, a sinner. I need your forgiveness and healing in my life. Thank you for your love for me that never grows cold.

What area of wrongdoing have you recently confessed to the Lord? Which of your relationships currently need healing?

16. LIKE FATHERS, LIKE SONS

*[David] said, "O my son Absalom, my son, my son Absalom! Would I
had died instead of you, O Absalom, my son, my son!"*
—2 Samuel 18:33

Scripture: 2 Samuel 18:9-33

For years I resented certain habits of my father. Finally, though, I realized that what I tended not to like in him were characteristics in me.
When I became a father, the knowledge that my son would likely grow
up to be like me in many ways seemed both encouraging and discour-
aging. I wanted him to have my good traits, such as they are, but not
my bad traits.

To his sorrow David discovers that his son Absalom shares traits with
his father that lead to his untimely, violent death. He follows in his
father's footsteps as a military leader and has his enemies killed. Absalom
even leads a revolt against David. When Absalom dies, his long hair
caught in the branches of a great oak, David mourns and wishes he had
died instead.

Leaders at a men's retreat I attended in 1992 invited us to talk about
our experiences of violence. I wept as I shared my remorse over having
hit my son, under 9 at the time. I feared that he would imitate me and
act out violently when he was older. While he has not, I had to learn
to forgive myself and place my son in God's hands.

Being faithful models to our children and seeking forgiveness when
we fail are difficult. Yet this pattern of living is something we can pass
on to our children, with God's help.

—Gordon Houser

*O God, I place the children in my life into your hands. Forgive me where I
have failed to be a good model for them.*

When have the children in your care caused you anguish? What traits,
good and bad, have you passed on to them?

17. THE GEHAZI SYNDROME

Gehazi . . . thought, "My master has let that Aramean Naaman off too
lightly . . . I will run after him and get something out of him."
—2 Kings 5:20

Scripture: 2 Kings 5:19-27

Let's face it: When it comes to the relationship between faith and money, none of us has all the answers. I wrote a booklet on the subject (*The Meaning of Tough: Wealth and Power*, Faith & Life Resources, 2003). But I never have a day when I am not uneasy or uncertain about how money should be used, given, spent, invested, or saved.

That's why I am not eager to sneer at Gehazi, the servant of Elisha, who sees in the free healing of the foreign military commander Naaman a missed opportunity. After all, Naaman has begged Elisha to accept a token of his gratitude. Gehazi is practically allowing the proud man to save face. And think what good can be done for God with a talent of silver! We wouldn't have to look long at the history of the Christian church, or the practices of some Christian organizations—perhaps even our own congregation—to find examples of the Gehazi Syndrome.

Right thinking about money and faith begins with the startling fact that God's gifts are just that: priceless and free. Money can accomplish and express many things, but God has everything to give us, and nothing is for sale. And just when I'm done struggling with the latest money question, I fall into the arms of awareness that grace is one of those free gifts.

—Leonard Beechy

You shower me with love and forgiveness without limit and without price.
Generous God, let me offer these things to others in the same way.

When do you find yourself doing God's work for your own profit—in money, status, approval? What helps you to keep your motivations straight?

18. PRACTICING THE MYSTERY OF PRAYER

[The Lord said,] "I have heard your prayer, I have seen your tears; indeed, I will heal you; on the third day you shall go up to the house of the Lord."
—2 Kings 20:5

Scripture: 2 Kings 20:1-11

When our 5-year-old son Jacob began to have frequent seizures, we prayed a lot. There was a special prayer service at our church for him; friends and neighbors prayed. In the end the doctor prescribed the right medicine, and today Jacob is a healthy and happy 9-year-old. Our prayers seemed to be answered.

But God's answers to prayer are not always so simple. Other parents who prayed over their children in that same hospital experienced the death of their child.

How does prayer work? It seems to work for Hezekiah. He prays for his health to be restored, and God grants that to him. In addition, God gives him another fifteen years of health so that he can serve God. But other biblical characters, including the apostle Paul, are not granted their requests (2 Corinthians 12:8-10).

Why do some of our intercessory prayers have happy outcomes and others not? As the story of martyrs in the Bible and church history attests, it is not clear that good outcomes are always the result of "faithful living" or more earnest prayers.

Even though prayer is a great mystery, I continue to pray fervently for others and for myself, knowing that God does hear me out. God will hear my prayer of thanksgiving in good times. God will also hear my prayer of anger when things turn out bad. Whatever happens, I am in touch with God, which is prayer at its best: conversation in relationship.

—Allan Rudy-Froese

Lord, give me the words to bring to you when I am in need, when I am angry, and when I am thankful.

Who are you praying for today? What happens to your faith when the results are not what you pray for?

19. CHRISTIAN HEROES

Before him there was no king like him, who turned to the Lord with all his heart, with all his soul, and with all his might.—2 Kings 23:25a

Scripture: 2 Kings 23:21-25

A recent television show featured a contest in which otherwise ordinary people competed to appear as a superhero in a comic book. On the surface, the competition was as silly as it sounds, with over-the-top costumes and characters who gained their superpowers from talking on cell phones and playing video games. Yet the show also tapped into basic human desires to have and to be a hero.

The show brought to mind the men who were my heroes as I grew up: a youth sponsor who showed me how one could be a Christian and still have fun; a pastor who exemplified the gentle yet firm guidance of a shepherd; and an older gentleman who made a point of taking an interest in my life.

Like Josiah, these role models turned to God with all their heart, soul, and might. They invited me to participate in church life as a member of God's covenant people. Unlike contestants in the superhero competition, they were not interested in being noticed or drawing attention to themselves.

Too many pop culture idols fill the headlines today with their rebellion, promiscuity, violence, and self-promotion. Josiah's example helps us to see how godly men can become heroes through their faithfulness to God and Scripture. We don't need capes or superpowers, but we do need role models who are clothed with the power of faithfulness.

—Matt Hamsher

Thank you, Lord, for the godly heroes that have shaped our lives. Help me to be a hero for you today.

What has impressed you about the men who have been role models in your life? What qualities of a godly hero are you developing for those who look up to you?

20. HELP THEM UNDERSTAND

They read from the book, from the law of God, with interpretation. They gave the sense, so the people understood.—Nehemiah 8:8

Scripture: Nehemiah 8:2-8

I grew up in a churchgoing family that faithfully attended services several times a week. As a result, there was no lack of Bible teaching and spiritual emphasis in my life. Yet I can't say I was always listening. There were times when Bible stories and church events captured my attention, but I also experienced long stretches of indifference.

This changed when I reached my teens. After I finished grade school, we moved to Southern California, where certain events revived my spiritual interest. In my youth group I met several guys who were new Christians and excited about following Jesus. Our youth pastor played in a "Jesus music" band and taught us Scripture songs accompanied by guitar. Our group ventured out weekly to witness and serve others in various ways. All these things spoke faith to me in new and exciting ways.

Under Ezra's leadership, the Jews experience the beginnings of spiritual revival when they return to their homeland after years of exile. Much has been lost regarding the understanding and following of God's ways. Ezra sees a need to reconnect the people with their faith, and works hard to accomplish that.

In many ways, our culture is parallel to Ezra's. We have roots of faith, but many have lost interest in and connection with their Creator. Simply reading God's Word and holding church services will not be enough to bring people back. As Ezra did in his day, we too must communicate faith in ways that are relevant and real to the current generation, so the people will "understand."

—Philip Wiebe

God, I want your presence to be real to me through your Word and through all your powerful works. Help me share your love in ways that will connect with and captivate those around me.

Where does God want your spiritual "head knowledge" to translate into daily action? Are you living your faith in ways that are intriguing to others?

21. WISDOM FOR SOLO-MEN

Fools despise wisdom and instruction.—Proverbs 1:7

Scripture: Proverbs 1:1-7

At a funeral I conducted in British Columbia, I met Guy, a deep-sea diver and paratrooper. This adventurer had recently gained distinction by piloting a sailboat alone for almost a year from Vancouver, around South America, Africa, and Australia, then up past Hawaii and home again—touching land only once!

At the travelogue I attended at Vancouver Yacht Club, he reported on his "schooling" en route. He read 80 books, some twice. And weather analysis was a constant lesson. One slide revealed ominous clouds over the bow. Guy asked us, "Seeing that, what do you do?"

"Tack away!" shore-huggers and landlubbers cried. "Nope," he replied. "Sail into it!" "Foolish!" we gasped. "Why?"

"Water," said the wind-worn Guy. "Wisdom at sea says to sail away from typhoons. But welcome other storms when your fresh water is low."

Guy avoided his own funeral by observing survival rules. Solomon, too, knows that great insight saves body, and soul. Solomon embraces the God of all understanding, and shares what he has learned in proverbs. Centuries later, he still gives us wisdom.

Guy inspired me to venture more in life, and to speak or write about what I discover. Today I proclaim that Solomon offers ever fresh wisdom—the water that men (especially those who travel solo) need for this tough life of journeys, tasks, and temptations.

What's your wisdom? Let a brother know. Only "fools" ignore lessons from others.

—Doug Schulz

My deepest thanks, Lord, for helping me learn and grow. And thanks for giving me grace, protection, and forgiveness when I've ignored wisdom. Help me guide others well.

In what hemisphere of life do you most need wisdom now? If you could write a proverb to reflect wisdom you've gained in life, what would it say?

22. IN PRAISE OF MY BELOVED

How graceful are your feet in sandals, O queenly maiden! Your rounded thighs are like jewels, the work of a master hand.—Song of Solomon 7:1

Scripture: Song of Solomon 7:1-9

This Bible passage may make us blush—not so much because of its highly charged and erotic language, but more because we cannot imagine saying such things, even to the one we love.

We have been socialized against such high-flown language. For the older generation, such language may seem unmanly and far too flowery to be spoken. Younger generations of men were discouraged from using language that seems to portray women merely as sexual objects. We've been taught, and rightly so, that love is more than sexual attraction. And so Solomon makes us blush. He sounds so old-fashioned.

Perhaps, though, we ought to reconsider. Many of us who are married said on our wedding day that God has brought us together. Our relationship is, first of all, a gift from God, a gift that we'll be exploring for a lifetime.

The gift is much more than sexual union. But what happens in the bedroom is a gift from God in which we revel as we grow deeper in love. It is striking that traditional Christian language for marriage is "becoming one flesh." Although "one flesh" may be a euphemism for intercourse, "becoming" points toward a lifelong journey of growth in love.

We may find Solomon's words a bit rich for our taste, or a bit old school. But let's not lose sight of the wonderful gift we've been given. And let's remember to speak words of love and appreciation, in the bedroom and everywhere else, in praise of our beloved. She is God's gift.

—Ron Adams

God, I thank you for the gift of my beloved. Free me to speak of the wonder of our love gladly and often.

When was the last time you sang the praises of your beloved? How can you be more intentional about expressing gratitude for such a gift?

23. UNCLEAN LIPS

The seraph touched my mouth . . . and said: "Now that this has touched your lips, your guilt has departed and your sin is blotted out."—Isaiah 6:7

Scripture: Isaiah 6:1-8

One of my good friends has recently begun a second career as a stand-up comedian. As a Christian, he has a routine that is both hilarious and clean. However, one of the occupational hazards of spending so much time in comedy clubs today is the amount of profanity, put-downs, sexual innuendo, and references to drug abuse that passes for humor. After one recent show the barrage of tasteless jokes was so bad that I felt like taking a shower as soon as it was over.

Have you ever felt uncomfortable after hearing an off-color joke or being in a conversation peppered with profanity? I wonder if Isaiah feels something similar when he cries out, "Woe is me! I am lost, for I am a man of unclean lips, and I live among a people of unclean lips" (v. 5). In full view of God's holiness, such language can make us feel unworthy, even guilty.

People say that talk is cheap. And that is true when our words do not match our actions. But words can also be powerful shapers of our lives and our relationship with God. They have the power to conjure up impure thoughts or encourage us to think instead on what is true, honorable, and pure (Philippians 4:8).

Thankfully, God stands ready to anoint our lips, to blot out our sin, to separate us from our sin, and to prepare us for holy service in the name of the Lord.

—Matt Hamsher

Anoint my lips, Lord, to speak your truth. Purify me of my sin so I might better serve you.

How have the words of others affected your life? How might God's anointing touch and change what comes out of your own mouth?

24. READY TO TRY AGAIN

[The Lord said,] "Take another scroll and write on it all the former words that were in the first scroll."—Jeremiah 36:28

Scripture: Jeremiah 36:27-32

As I look back on many years of serving churches in worship, teaching, and leadership, I would say the efforts have mostly been rewarding. But there have been times when I was ready to give up. Usually these involved instances where I felt the ministry made no difference. As leaders, we sensed God's calling for a certain direction or task, yet our labors seemed only to inspire grumbling.

Jeremiah must often feel that. He is a prophet who faces continual resistance to his messages. Today's reading describes what happens after God has instructed Jeremiah to write a scroll with warnings "against Israel and Judah and all the nations," so they would "turn from their evil ways" and find forgiveness (36:2-3).

Once again, Jeremiah's message hasn't gone over well. King Jehoiakim burns the scroll and tries to have Jeremiah arrested. But the matter is far from over. Now God tells Jeremiah to write the scroll again, this time adding warnings of punishment for the hard-hearted king.

This couldn't be fun for Jeremiah. At times he complains to God about his ongoing difficulties and lack of success as a prophet. Yet Jeremiah always dusts himself off and continues to do the work God has given.

I want to do that too. I need God's strength to help me keep going in my vocation, especially through the tough times. And when God calls me to pick up a task that may have failed before, I want to be ready to try again.

—Philip Wiebe

I really try to serve you, Lord, but sometimes it just doesn't seem to work. I need your help! I want to keep following your call, even when times get tough.

Do you need to seek God's strength in a difficult area of service right now? Is there a calling you've given up on that you should consider taking up again?

25. COURAGE TO SPEAK UP

[Ebed-melech said,] "These men have acted wickedly in all they did to the prophet Jeremiah by throwing him into the cistern to die there of hunger."
—Jeremiah 38:9

Scripture: Jeremiah 38:7-13

It takes courage to speak up on behalf of justice and mercy. At the time of today's story (about 588 BC), Jeremiah prophesies that the city of Jerusalem will shortly fall to the power of the Babylonians. The king and his governing officials are upset with the prophet's words. Fearing that Jeremiah's message will demoralize the population, they confine him to a vaulted cell in a dungeon (37:16). Later, they throw him into a cistern (38:6). Ebed-Melech, a foreign official in the royal palace, speaks to the king on behalf of Jeremiah.

Like the people of ancient Judah, Christians in North America are currently caught in a tense political environment, whose chief concern is security. There are sharply different opinions about the best way to provide national security. To voice an opinion against the military initiatives, for example, may be viewed as antipatriotic.

In such times, Christian peacemakers must find ways to support the government while opposing unjust actions in war. We need the courage of Ebed-Melech to step up to this challenge. He speaks directly to the king, the one who can initiate remedial action. He minces no words; he says the men have "acted wickedly" against Jeremiah. And God grants him favor. The king responds to his concern and lets Ebed-Melech rescue Jeremiah.

May God grant each of us the courage to speak up as Ebed-Melech does, even when we fear what might happen to us.

—Ervin Stutzman

God, grant us wisdom and courage in the face of worries about our security. Help us live with the assurance of your protection.

In what ways does God call Christians to speak to the "powers that be"? How does God call us to support the prophets who speak up against ruling authorities?

26. EAT YOUR VEGETABLES

[Daniel asked,] "Let us be given vegetables to eat and water to drink."
—Daniel 1:12

Scripture: Daniel 1:1-20

As a new Christian at age 15, I did not know other Christians who might teach me about the faith. But I knew I should read the Bible, even though it seemed difficult to understand. One evening I read this passage and thought that I should be a vegetarian.

I gave up eating meat for a while, but it bothered my mother, who made our family's meals. So I gave up my vegetarianism. Later, at the end of college and for several years thereafter, I avoided meat again, except when I visited my family; I didn't want to make it too big an issue. When I married the daughter of a farmer who raised beef cattle, however, I decided to give it up.

Eventually I learned that the point of Daniel's story is not that we should become vegetarian but to be faithful to God. We are not to "defile [ourselves] with the royal rations of food and wine" (v. 8). Our food may not come from idol worshippers, but as Eric Schlosser shows in the book *Fast Food Nation*, it is sometimes tainted by the injustices associated with large corporate interests. We are called to glorify God in all that we do, including our eating habits (see *Good Eating*, by Stephen H. Webb).

Our choices about what we eat affect our health and can show love for others. Since my wife was diagnosed with cancer in November 2006, we have been eating healthier, including avoiding red meat. However we eat, let us do it in love.

—Gordon Houser

God, I want all I do, including my diet, to bring glory to you.

How healthy is your diet? How do your eating habits affect others?

27. PENETRATING THE DARKNESS

[Nebuchadnezzar said,] "I . . . lifted my eyes to heaven, and my reason returned to me."—Daniel 4:34

Scripture: Daniel 4:28-37

When I've been "down," I've battled my melancholy with prayer, counseling, and kind companionship. But many victims of depression find prayer impossible. The stuff of church life even feels like a spiritual fraud, shallow and flaky, seeming to harbor more judgment than gentle understanding. Clearly, we need accurate knowledge about deep depression and mental illness, so that genuine sensitivity marks how we respond to those who suffer most severely.

King Nebuchadnezzar, it appears, has entered his place of shadows through a gate he has opened himself. Self-absorbed with his absolute power, he loses perspective on human limitations. His ego swells, swallowing his reason, and his reverence for a Higher Power vanishes. The arrogant man is diminished to a dull animal state.

This alarming account is, in part, a warning. Self-centeredness that drifts into total disregard for God's sovereignty over life has consequences (v. 32). But this story doesn't advocate labeling depressed persons (myself included) as bleak souls deserving their darkness. Instead, it points to a brighter conclusion.

God does not leave the picture when a man descends into deep shadows, even if he has brought despair on himself. God comprehends spiritual and emotional suffering. Our darkness itself serves as an invitation to "lift [our] eyes to heaven" (v. 34). Then we see that restoration to health is God's priority, so that with a clear mind we appreciate, as the rejuvenated king does, that "all [God's] works are truth, and his ways are justice" (37).

Sometimes our minds and souls are darkened. But God's light penetrates.

—Doug Schulz

Let me see light today, Lord. Let me be light. Lead me to bright roads, and let me gently guide others out of gloomy places.

What brightness in my life could I share with someone as an inspiration for them today? What gloomy thing might I ask a friend to pray about?

28. THE PROPHET AND THE PROSTITUTE

In the place where it was said to them, "You are not my people," it shall be said to them, "Children of the living God."—Hosea 1:10

Scripture: Hosea 1

As a musician, I watch the occasional music awards show to see new singers and bands who are finding fame. Sometimes the words of the winning artists surprise me. "I want to give glory to God," they may say, or "I thank Jesus my Savior." I tend to react with a bit of shock. "This woman is praising God while wearing *that?*" Or, "He made *that* album and is now thanking Jesus?"

Today's reading reminds me to be careful in my judgment about the faith of others. Who am I to question the presence and work of God in their lives? If I didn't know that Hosea's story was from the Bible, I would be highly skeptical of it. After all, God tells the prophet to marry a prostitute and "have children of whoredom" (v. 2). What's that all about? I can only imagine the uproar if a Christian leader was involved in such a scenario today.

But God has a purpose. The message needs to get out that Israel has acted like a prostitute in following other gods. God calls Hosea to demonstrate this in a daring and dramatic way.

Too often I have tunnel vision regarding God's presence and methods. Yet God can work through the marriage of a prophet and a prostitute, as well as through flamboyant celebrities who surprisingly give God glory. God can even work dramatically in me. If God would lead me to serve in some daring way in my world, I want to be ready and willing.

—Philip Wiebe

God, forgive me for my limited vision of how you work in the world. Help me see your power and love where I haven't noticed it before, even in me.

Is there some situation or person you need to change your mind about, acknowledging that God is at work in them? How might God be calling you to do something daring or different?

29. ORDINARY PEOPLE

Amos answered Amaziah, "I am no prophet, nor a prophet's son; but I am a herdsman, and a dresser of sycamore trees."—Amos 7:14

Scripture: Amos 7:10-17

My father was no prophet. He finished eighth grade; then he was needed on his family's dairy farm. For the rest of his working life, he remained a farmer, and he also drove a ready-mix concrete truck to pay bills and to support his five children through college.

He taught a men's Sunday school class and used this forum to air his strongest convictions. The educated elite, he said, were perpetuating their own institutions at the expense of mission efforts. Love, not education, he said, is the church's reason for being. Sometimes I agreed with him, sometimes not. Until he died in 1988, his message was the same.

Amos, a farmer from the south, appears at Israel's main worship center, Bethel, with no credentials. He has only the word of the Lord, and that word is bad news. Israel has wealth, places of worship, military might—but it does not have justice. The poor suffer in the economy and in the courts. As a result, Israel is about to suffer destruction and exile. No wonder the official prophets move quickly to silence this bumpkin.

My father and 32 years of teaching high school students have taught me at least one thing: There are no ordinary people. The minute we label someone as "ordinary," we discover that they possess some extraordinary truth. We may or may not have ears to hear this truth, but it is no less the word of the Lord. The trick is not to label, but to listen.

—Leonard Beechy

Lord, your word may come to me through people and circumstances I am not expecting. Help me to hold off on labeling, and to listen for an extraordinary word from you.

What "qualifications" do I require before I lend someone my attention and respect? What qualifications does God require to deliver a prophetic word?

30. WHEN THINGS DO NOT END WELL

God changed his mind about the calamity that he said he would bring upon [the Ninevites]. . . . But this was very displeasing to Jonah.
—Jonah 3:10; 4:1

Scripture: Jonah 4

The book of Jonah does not end well. Jonah remains angry as the Ninevites revel in God's mercy. Even though, with the shade tree and worm, God tries to show Jonah demonstrations why he is being merciful, Jonah still sulks and wishes to die. The story ends almost humorously as God lectures the prophet about God's divine right to save these 120,000 people—and their animals! We hear no response from Jonah. The story does not end well, at least for him.

Some events in our lives simply do not end well. We may have said something to a sibling, friend, or spouse that we can never take back. We may have tried to forgive someone, but as hard as we try, we are lost in pain and anger. We recall a romantic relationship that went wrong.

A poem I recently heard may help Jonah and us as we face endings that we can no longer affect or change. "What's done is done; let it be. What's been left undone, has been left undone; let it be."

Just as at the end of the day we have to admit that we did not get through all we needed to do today and must "let it be," so there are times in our lives when we must simply let go, move on, and trust God's mercy to take care of the ending.

—Allan Rudy-Froese

God, grant me wisdom to know when I must let some things be. Help me to leave the control of the outcome to you.

What are the things that have not ended well for you? What are the steps that you can take to "let it be"?

31. MORE THAN A NAME

Her husband Joseph, being a righteous man and unwilling to expose her to public disgrace, planned to dismiss her quietly.—Matthew 1:19

Scripture: Matthew 1:18-25

I know a man whose ego is in constant need of stroking. Many of us, of course, need to be reassured of our value, especially in the eyes of those we hold in high regard. This fellow's need seems deeper than that. He cannot afford to be anything less than right.

His need for affirmation becomes especially ugly when he tries to satisfy it by demeaning someone else. His friends often cringe as he speaks badly of a neighbor or a co-worker. Blind to his impact on others, my friend does whatever it takes to prop up his reputation.

My friend's tragic flaw is not uncommon among men. Though not to the same degree, we find it tempting to seek advantage for ourselves at others' expense. Our reputation in the community, at church, or at work can become something we protect at all costs, even at the cost of hurting or diminishing others.

Joseph's uncommon decency speaks to those of us whose reputations come first. He, too, has a reputation to protect. He cannot bring himself to stay with Mary after hearing news of her pregnancy. But even before the angel comes, Joseph is unwilling to denounce Mary. Instead, he decides to break off with her quietly. And then the angel comes and calls Joseph to something even greater.

This story reveals that love and mercy are more valuable than a good name. That might seem out of step with contemporary male culture. But it is the way of Jesus.

—Ron Adams

Jesus, fill me with the wisdom of Joseph. Help me to hold my ego in check, and to regard love and mercy as greater than my reputation.

When are you tempted to raise yourself up by diminishing others? What can you do today to put love and mercy ahead of your need for approval?

32. PARTY TIME!

[Jesus said,] "Go and learn what this means, 'I desire mercy, not sacrifice.' For I have come to call not the righteous but sinners." —Matthew 9:13

Scripture: Matthew 9:9-13

One of the best things that has ever happened to me was becoming a father. After my first child was born, I walked on air for days. People could tell that something wonderful had happened to me, and I wasn't shy about telling them about the miracle of new life that God had given to me and my wife. I wanted to shout it from the rooftops and tell everyone just how special my daughter was.

I soon realized that this gift was also a big responsibility and required a lot of sacrifices. I had to endure sleep-deprived nights, temper tantrums, and sibling rivalries. Being a father has been a lot of work, but all it takes is one unprompted hug or "I love you, Dad" to fill me with the joy I had at the beginning, all over again.

We can experience our Christian faith in similar ways. Too often the exuberance of our initial commitment to God and our experience of God's mercy can seem to drown in the sacrifices we make. Like the Pharisees at Jesus' dinner party with "sinners," we can become locked into the expectations of others and serving only out of a sense of duty.

We need to be role models, and we need to serve God, but we also need moments when we relive, celebrate, and tell others of the freshness of those early days when Jesus first called to us, "Follow me."

—Matt Hamsher

O Lord, help me today to remember the joy I felt when I first decided to follow you.

When have you experienced the joy of following Jesus? How might that joy reorder your responsibilities today? How can you share it with others?

33. THE BENEFIT OF DOUBT

[John asked,] "Are you the one who is to come, or are we to wait for another?"—Matthew 11:3

Scripture: Matthew 11:1-11

Sitting in prison, John the Baptist has lots of time to think. His disciples are reporting on Jesus' activities of healing, feeding, giving good news to the poor. Yet these don't exactly fit the picture John's preaching has painted of the Messiah. John has preached that he will come carrying a winnowing fork, ready to burn the chaff of evil and evil-doers "with unquenchable fire" (Matthew 3:11).

John has baptized Jesus and launched his ministry. Now, watching through a prison window well, he has begun to wonder. With time running out on his own life, he decides that it won't hurt to ask.

The theologian Paul Tillich once said, "Doubt isn't the opposite of faith; it is an element of faith." If that is true, then the faith of John the Baptist is very much alive. Jesus certainly isn't offended by John's question. He simply tells John's messengers to take back to John an eyewitness report, couched in language from Isaiah that John will easily recognize.

There are at least two lessons here: For one, Jesus is able to receive our doubts and questions, which actually seem to keep our faith alive. For another, when it comes to faith, the best explanation is demonstration of the things we have seen and heard.

—Leonard Beechy

Lord, I believe; help my unbelief. Accept my imperfect faith. Let me look not so much for proof for my beliefs, as for signs of your activity.

Have you experienced doubts that led to growth? When you're looking for where God is at work in the world, what signs "give it away"?

34. NO LICENSE TO CURSE

*[Jesus] said to [the fig tree], "May no fruit ever come from you again!"
And [it] withered at once.—Matthew 21:18*

Scripture: Matthew 21:18-22

Expressions of cursing and swearing serve as a common outlet for anger or frustration in many of our workplaces. In today's reading, Jesus curses a fig tree—the only occasion when he uses his miraculous power to destroy a living organism. Is it because he is upset that he can't find something to eat? Or that the tree is barren?

But something deeper is happening in this story. Many Bible scholars see the fig tree as a symbol of the nation of Israel (see Hosea 9:10; Nahum 3:12). The barren fig tree stands for something more than the denial of a roadside snack.

Jesus' harsh words to the tree are a dramatized parable exposing the barrenness Jesus sees in the temple area of Jerusalem. His action announces the way Jerusalem will wither and fall in AD 70, when the Romans conquer the city and destroy its defenders. Not long after cursing the fig tree, Jesus pronounces seven woes on the Pharisees and teachers of the law (Matthew 23).

So do Jesus' pronouncements justify similar "cursing" in our lives? Unless we have Jesus' insight into God's plans, we do better not to pronounce woes, even when we are angry. Scripture also urges us to bless, and not curse those who do us wrong (Romans 12:14).

—Ervin Stutzman

God, help me to refrain from cursing the people that you have invited me to bless, even in the face of anger and frustration.

If Jesus were walking among us in person today, what might he curse, if anything? Under what circumstances, if any, is it appropriate to call down God's judgment on objects, living things, or other people?

35. DON'T EVEN GO THERE

Jesus . . . said, "Why are you putting me to the test?"—Matthew 22:18b

Scripture: Matthew 22:15-22

People often say that one should avoid discussing religion and politics in group situations, due to the volatile nature of these subjects. In my own experience, religion isn't so hard to talk about. Many are happy to discuss spiritual matters and are searching for deeper meaning in life.

Politics are another matter, however. In our divisive ideological climate, even a bit of such talk gets people fuming and red-faced. That's why I tend to be evasive when political discussions come up. As a follower of Jesus, my politics do not fit neatly into any right- or left-leaning agenda. Getting dragged into ideology fights can be a trap that squeezes big matters of faith into small-minded human schemes.

Jesus sees this in a political question that some religious teachers pose to him. Is it right for God's people to pay taxes to the emperor, a false god? Jesus doesn't directly answer their "test" question. Instead, he digs down to the real issue. Jesus goes right past their inquiry to issue a challenge: "It isn't wrong to give to the emperor what is the emperor's, but are you also giving to God the things that are God's?"

Jesus would ask the same of us. There are times when our strong opinions about political and other controversial issues can actually hinder the sharing and pursuit of more important matters of faith. I want to set those kinds of distractions aside and truly give God the things that are God's.

—Philip Wiebe

Lord, help me avoid the endless controversies and tangled arguments that can distract me and others from finding true faith in you. I want to give you all that's yours.

How could your expression of political views distract others from finding faith? How might you help to heal a relationship by diffusing a needless argument?

36. YOU CAN'T WASTE GRACE

Jesus . . . said, "She has performed a good service for me."
—Matthew 26:10

Scripture: Matthew 26:6-13

Is it better to give or to receive? Many of us believe that generously serving others is our mission as men. It is faith's watermark—love shown true in a self-absorbed world. But receiving is a form of witness, too, as today's story demonstrates in remarkable fashion.

Jesus is a guest. Good heavens! His host is a leper! (v. 6). Receiving hospitality here, Jesus honors a likely outcast. He shows Simon's worth to God, who loves those deemed unclean and sinful.

Further, Jesus receives protection. His enemies are about to kill him (v. 4). By eating here with an untouchable, Jesus affirms that we're doing God's will, whether we host the helpless or grace the table of society's "rejects." Either way, we're making tangible acts of compassion our life's urgent work. It's God's grace on display.

Then there is the woman. Jesus smells death near. Perhaps she sees him shudder at imagined pain. Then he smells something so different, so sweet. She pours. He receives the perfume, absorbing extravagant comfort. He welcomes her sensuous action, better now than a generic act of donating cash to the numberless poor.

Then, shockingly, Jesus declares her a worldwide icon! In a time when women don't count, except to serve men and receive little credit, he blesses her as his most noteworthy disciple. He receives her absolutely.

So, give or receive? Jesus says: "Let God's sweet grace be real. Show it. Know it. Share it. Feel it. Want it. Love it."

—Doug Schulz

Lord, what can I do to comfort you? Show me how to be more gracious and receptive, giving and receiving in your name.

Do you practice a balance of generosity in giving and celebration of receiving? How can you appropriately honor those who model these features of grace?

37. PAY ATTENTION

[Jesus] said to Peter, "So, could you not stay awake with me one hour? . . . The spirit indeed is willing, but the flesh is weak."—Matthew 26:40-41

Scripture: Matthew 26:36-46

When it comes to our spiritual lives, we're our own worst enemies. At least I am. For the times I want to be most attentive to God, most attuned to the pattern of my life, I so often choose moments when I am least up to the task. I read or write at night until I can't anymore, then try to pray. Or I try the morning, when my mind keeps leaping from the holy present moment to the tasks of the day that lie ahead. Amazingly, God often honors these scraps of attention with genuine insight and the sense of divine presence. God is more attentive to me than I am to God.

Matthew presents the disciples of Jesus as bad examples of prayer. Even the Big Three—Peter, James, and John—fail Jesus in the simple task of staying awake. Jesus has made himself vulnerable to them, confessed his anxiety and grief, and admitted that he needs something from them. It is not heroism or blood or sacrifice that he needs. It is nothing but their companionship, their presence, their attention. Even in this, they fail him.

I take comfort in Jesus' gracious response to them: He is saddened, but still invites them on the next leg of the journey with him. Chances are that today Jesus has no need of your heroism or blood or sacrifice. Just for today, for this moment, Jesus needs your companionship, your presence, your attention. Can you give him that?

—Leonard Beechy

You give me life, Lord, and you ask for my companionship. Right now, in these moments, I will remain here and stay awake with you.

Think of times when your friends have let you down or disappointed you. How have you responded? What light might these experiences shed on your companionship with God?

38. MOUNTAINTOP VISIONS—SWEET BUT SHORT

Peter said to Jesus, "Rabbi, it is good for us to be here; let us make three dwellings, one for you, one for Moses, and one for Elijah."—Mark 9:5

Scripture: Mark 9:2-10

Several years ago while touring Israel/Palestine, I visited Mt. Tabor, the traditional site of Jesus' transfiguration. The solitary peak rewards Jesus, Peter, James, and John with a majestic view after their arduous climb to the top. Here, far above the farmers going about their daily chores and traffic passing on the plain below, the disciples leave worldly cares behind to hear from God in the midst of a miracle.

Today a church sits on the site of the transfiguration, and inside there is a beautiful worship space. How ironic, though, that the church has two chapels off to the side, one dedicated to Moses and another to Elijah. Here, after all these years, Peter's impetuous wish has finally been fulfilled.

Although it is entirely human to try to preserve a holy moment of contact with God, it still seems a mistake for Peter to suggest that they stay up on the mountaintop, or try to make the moment last forever. God often blesses us with mountaintop experiences of our own. But for us, as for Peter, it is a mistake to think we can dwell in them forever.

Eventually we must come down off the mountain because our tasks remain unfinished. Nor can we exercise control over our spiritual experiences. But we can give ourselves over to them when they come, appreciating their promise of future glory.

—Matt Hamsher

Thank you, Lord, for the many ways you have shown yourself to me in the past. Help me to live today in the light of the promise of your resurrection.

What "mountaintop experiences" of God's presence have you experienced in the past? How have they provided hope and trust in God for trials that came later?

39. ONE THING

Jesus, looking at [the man], loved him and said, "You lack one thing."
—Mark 10:21

Scripture: Mark 10:17-27

After I graduated from university, I joined an intentional Christian community whose members pooled all their money and lived from a "common purse." One of my motivations stemmed from this passage. I wanted to follow Jesus' command to give away what I had. As a 22-year-old, though, I didn't have much.

Before I joined this community, a college friend told me that he knew someone who had made a similar commitment and "was not the same person." That scared me. It turned out that living this way helped us live more intensely our common desire to follow Jesus' way. That meant being honest with each other, confessing our sins, and learning to love each other as we were, not as we tried to present ourselves. It was difficult but rewarding.

Only Mark's version of this story says that Jesus loves him. He must be moved by the man's desire to be faithful. The man must seem to have it all: money and morals. But Jesus says he lacks "one thing." Only one? That seems good.

Richard Rohr describes "two ways of being a prophet. One is to tell the enslaved that they can be free. It is the difficult path of Moses. The second is to tell those who think they are free that they are in fact enslaved. This is the even more difficult path of Jesus." Jesus loves the rich man enough to tell him that he is enslaved to his possessions. He gives the man an opportunity choose a life-giving path.

—Gordon Houser

What do you ask of me, Lord, in order to follow you? Help me to be faithful to your call.

Take inventory of how your possessions, career ambitions, or other preoccupations may be enslaving you. What is the "one thing" you lack in your walk with Jesus?

40. TAKING ADVANTAGE OF EXILE

[The angel to Zechariah:] "You will be mute, unable to speak, until the day these things occur." —Luke 1:20

Scripture: Luke 1:8-21, 57-61

I wonder what it sounds like at first. Zechariah probably wants to say something like, "For Real! A baby!" But the sound gets caught in his throat and comes out sounding like a funny cough—or perhaps like the braying of his donkey.

Zechariah is struck dumb until the child will be born. Hardly a fair thing to do to an expectant father! But I like to think that Zechariah takes advantage of this odd exile from human conversation. Perhaps he studies the Psalms during his exile, looking for just the right words to recite when his baby is born (see Luke 1:67-79).

In our own lives, we go through exiles of various sorts. It may be the loss of a job, or the tragic loss of a friend. We may slip into a depression or become ill for a time. Regardless of the severity of our exile, these can be times to reflect on our lives, or perhaps to do some new things.

A friend who lost his job happily started retraining for a trade that he had always wanted to do. Another friend who suffered from depression sang hymns and learned to knit. He literally sang and knitted his way out of his dark exile.

When we go into exile, it is easy for us to feel sorry for ourselves. But those who reach the place where they see exile as an opportunity, come out refreshed and, like Zechariah, singing a new song.

—Allan Rudy-Froese

God, thank you for the exiles that I have had in my life. Help me to notice and to be an encouragement for those who go into exile.

What did you do in your last exile? What are some of the ways that we as men can support one another when our lives are turned upside down?

41. ARE YOU READY?

It had been revealed to [Simeon] by the Holy Spirit that he would not see death before he had seen the Lord's Messiah—Luke 2:26

Scripture: Luke 2:25-35

As a college student I studied Leo Tolstoy's novel *The Death of Ivan Ilyich*, where a man desperately seeks life's meaning before he dies. Tolstoy wrote this story to reveal the hope he'd found through his conversion.

Shortly after reading *Ivan Ilyich*, I visited my folks. My father pulled me aside, whispering, "I'm going to die this year." Thirteen years earlier, at 63, he'd had a heart attack and was given five years or less to live.

My eyes swam. "You're sure, Dad?" I said. His blue eyes were pure and unyielding as he nodded. "Are you ready?" I managed. His "yes" rang clear as cracking ice on the big slough down the hill, where he had taught me to skate. "I love this life," he said. "Every day I see is God's gift. But now I'll see him. I'm glad for that." Two months later, after a severe stroke, he did see God.

The Holy Spirit tells old Simeon that he will see the Christ before he dies. Picture this frail pilgrim holding the infant, facing the parents, and speaking about seeing God's "salvation" (v. 30). After all that Mary and Joseph have been through, imagine what powerful purpose those words give them—a vision to endure all things to come.

Alfred Lord Tennyson said: "Knowledge comes, but wisdom lingers." Men like Simeon, seeking through their last years to know God, bless us with their insight.

—Doug Schulz

Thanks, Lord, for the deeper vision, faith, and hope inspired by older men. Teach me how to pass on insight humbly and eagerly, as I direct others toward you.

Who are the men who have most influenced you to be focused on a faith that's real and alive? What particular word of wisdom do you need from them now?

42. MAKING THE PASS

[John said,] "One who is more powerful than I is coming."—Luke 3:16

Scripture: Luke 3:15-18

Michael Jordan's highest one-game scoring total was an amazing 69 points, against the Cleveland Cavaliers in 1990. In the same game, rookie forward Stacey King hit a free throw. After the game, King told reporters, "I'll always remember this as the game Michael Jordan and I combined for seventy points."

King's joke takes on more meaning in the context of Jordan's career. At the time, the Bulls coach Phil Jackson was persuading Jordan that the Bulls could win an NBA championship only if the superstar channeled more of his talents toward making his teammates better. In 1991 the Bulls won the first of six NBA championships.

From all accounts, it's clear that in first century Palestine, John the Baptist is a big deal. Josephus, a Jewish historian of the time, reports that John's popularity gets him jailed. Years after his death, the apostle Paul finds pockets of John's followers as far away as Ephesus (Acts 19:1-4). Such popularity must present John with temptations. Yet every account in the Gospels shows John deflecting the attention to his younger, milder cousin. In paintings over the centuries, the standard portrayal of John the Baptist is a man pointing toward Jesus.

From Michael Jordan and John the Baptist we learn that the most powerful thing we can ever do is to release power in others. This may mean stepping into the background, pointing attention away from ourselves, making the pass. But this way power isn't divided—it is multiplied.

—Leonard Beechy

Show me today, Lord, how to deflect attention from myself and release power in another person. In this way, may the attention be pointed ultimately toward you.

How have you been empowered by another person? What are some ways this can happen in "teams" that you belong to in the workplace, home, or church?

43. FAITH: HUMBLE AND BOLD

[The centurion said,] "I also am a man set under authority, with soldiers under me."—Luke 7:8

Scripture: Luke 7:1-10

Sometimes great faith rises up from unexpected quarters to amaze even the faithful. From the point of view of first-century Jews, the centurion of our story has three strikes against him: he is Gentile, Roman, and an officer in a repressive foreign army. But the God-fearing officer in this story loves the Jewish people and has built a synagogue for them. The Jewish leaders plead for Jesus to help him.

We can learn two things from the officer's actions. First, he doesn't plead for a miracle based on his own influence or worthiness. Rather, he states that he is not worthy for Jesus to step under his roof. He asks Jesus to "only speak the word" from where he is (v. 7). We need not "pull rank" in order to get God's attention. We do not need to impress God with our worthiness before God will act in our behalf.

Second, the officer expresses his faith by acknowledging Jesus' power and authority in the world. He uses a military analogy, likening Jesus' power over sickness to his own authority over soldiers in his army. This statement earns Jesus' admiration and commendation. This is one of two times when Jesus commends Gentiles for their great faith (see Matthew 15:28), and both involve the healing of the petitioner's child.

As we experience times when we sense a need for God's intervention, we do well to remember the centurion's secret to great faith: a sense of his own vulnerability and unworthiness before God, and at the same time, a declaration of God's immense power to heal.

—Ervin Stutzman

God, give me faith to always trust in you. Thank you for your goodness.

On what basis did Jesus decide that the centurion was worthy of his attention? What determines one's worth before God today?

44. BEYOND THE PIGEON HOLES

Jesus said to [Zacchaeus], "Today salvation has come to this house, because he too is a son of Abraham."—Luke 19:9

Scripture: Luke 19:1-10

I once sat in the back of a Sunday school room listening to a prison inmate and prison chaplain talk about spirituality and prison life. The inmate and the chaplain looked and sounded similar: both were dressed casually and both spoke well. A friend came in late, listened for a minute, and then asked me with some frustration, "Which one is the prisoner?" I told him to figure it out for himself. It took him ten minutes.

My friend expected something that would easily distinguish the "bad guy" from the "good guy." When he finally figured it out, he realized that his stereotype of "prisoner" would not hold. This man was not simply a prisoner but also a well-spoken brother in Christ, who was fun to be with.

Jesus is able to see with different eyes than those around him. He sees Zacchaeus, not simply as a short, morally slippery tax collector, but also as a "son of Abraham," who has great potential. Jesus habitually serves those who are often put into handy negative categories, showing that God sees us in all our potential as "sons" and "daughters."

Today when you hastily pigeonhole someone, remember Jesus' way of seeing. Try a short conversation with someone whom others view negatively, and thus continue the mission of Jesus.

—Allan Rudy-Froese

God, give me new names for those whom I have usually written off. Take the blinders off my eyes so that I might see people as your sons and daughters.

Who in our society tends to be written off because of prejudice and negative pigeonholing? What are some habits that can teach us to see with new eyes?

45. SECRET BIRTH

Nicodemus, who had at first come to Jesus by night, also came, bringing a mixture of myrrh and aloes.—John 19:39

Scripture: John 3:1-15; 19:39

I wonder if every class reunion has a story like Isaac's. This is the guy who, to everyone's complete surprise, has become not only a sincere and dedicated Christian, but also the pastor of a local church. At our last reunion, Isaac told how he lived only to play football, but then broke his leg in his senior year, canceling participation. This much I already knew.

What I didn't know is that the injury gave him two things: a crisis of purpose in life, and time to think about it. While his leg healed, Isaac bought a Bible. When he got to John's account of Jesus' conversation with Nicodemus, he stopped to pray, asking Jesus to make him new. At that time, none of his classmates knew about this. It took a few years for what was born that day to grow. But Isaac's strong, sincere testimony was proof of the mature new life that ultimately resulted.

So it must be with Nicodemus. A Pharisee, "a leader of the Jews," he comes to Jesus under the cover of night. Although their conversation is recorded, the immediate result is not. What we do know is that when, later in the story, we see Nicodemus again, he is taking risks for Jesus: speaking in his defense among his colleagues (7:50), and helping with his burial (19:39).

How many other Isaacs have been transformed by "overhearing" Jesus' conversation with Nicodemus? And how do you know what the results might be, even years later, of a conversation you have today?

—Leonard Beechy

God, make me alert to the possibility of any conversation becoming a holy moment, transforming me or my conversation partner.

Is it possible to be a "secret Christian"? Who do you know whose "new birth" had a long gestation period of quiet growth before it became public?

46. DOUBTS AND BLESSINGS

Thomas answered him, "My Lord and my God!"—John 20:28

Scripture: John 20:24-29

Thomas has been given a bum rap. Even the beloved disciple, John, doesn't believe Jesus has risen from the dead until he sees Jesus' burial clothes laid out and empty (John 20:8). Mary Magdalene thinks Jesus is the gardener until he speaks her name (20:16). The other disciples truly believe only after Jesus appears to them. But Thomas is the one we call "Doubting Thomas."

John tells this story to affirm the faith of later generations. As Jesus says, "Those who believe without seeing are blessed." But Thomas is also blessed. He receives what he has asked for. He sees the risen Jesus. Would that all our prayers were answered so completely!

Still, generations of Christians have treated Thomas as the spiritual weakling of the disciple band. Small wonder that we are so reluctant to express our doubts and fears to one another. This may be especially true of men. No matter how sophisticated we claim to be, we retain the images of perfect manhood taught by our culture. A real man is strong, confident, unwavering in conviction. A real man does not admit to doubt.

The story of Thomas, however, invites us to a different way of being. Jesus not only welcomes his doubts; he also answers them profoundly: "Put your finger here and see my hands" (v. 27). It is his honest journey with doubt that leads Thomas to proclaim that Jesus is Lord and God! (v. 28).

With Thomas as our example, let's stop pretending. Let's offer our doubts to Jesus.

—Ron Adams

Lord Jesus, you see through my façade of perfect manhood. Help me to tell you the truth today. Take my doubts and, through them, bring me closer to you.

What do you struggle to believe? How can you become more intentional today about sharing your doubts with Jesus?

47. FOLLOW THE SPIRIT'S NUDGES

The Spirit said to Philip, "Go over to this chariot and join it."
—Acts 8:29

Scripture: Acts 8:26-40

Not long ago, as I prepared to speak at a conference gathering, I sensed the Spirit of God nudging me to lead in a responsive prayer instead. Since I enjoy preaching, I resisted the idea and wrestled with God about it. Would people think I was shirking my duty? Once I followed the nudge, however, I knew that it was indeed God's will.

The story of Philip speaks of responsiveness to God's voice. While Philip may have hesitated to leave a successful ministry in Samaria, he follows the Lord's bidding into the desert. When he arrives there, the Spirit points him toward a high official from Ethiopia who is receptive to the gospel.

This encounter results in the first recorded conversion of a Gentile to Christian faith and thus also the first from Africa—the Ethiopian eunuch. Today, Ethiopians and other Africans trace their churches' dynamic witness to Philip's responsiveness to the Spirit.

At times when I pray, I wrestle to discern whether or not it is indeed the Spirit's voice urging me to certain actions. I often share such urges with my spouse, testing my hearing with her discernment. Such nudges have led me to do things I would otherwise have been hesitant to do. I have given more generously, taken greater risks for God's kingdom, and spoken more boldly. The Spirit rewards God's people for listening to these nudges.

—Ervin Stutzman

God, enable me to hear and respond to the voice of your Spirit in the midst of daily life.

Remember a time when you sensed God nudging you to do something you would not have done otherwise. How were you sure it was the Spirit of God speaking, rather than some other voice?

48. CHOOSE THE CHALLENGING OPTION

The Lord said to [Ananias], "Get up and go to the street called Straight, and at the house of Judas look for a man of Tarsus named Saul."
—Acts 9:11

Scripture: Acts 9:10-19

In some places around the world where Christianity is well established, churches are finding it increasingly difficult to evangelize the men of their culture. Men see church as a crutch, something for the weak to lean on, or a boring place where nothing much happens to make it worth their while.

In England, the Urban Mission Toolkit program responds to this reality by challenging men to participate in mission as an expression of their Christian faith. With the motto, "Love is a verb," participants overcome their fear of the inner city by volunteering in homeless shelters, soup kitchens, and other community organizations in urban centers. A greater ratio of men participate in the program in part because it recognizes that successfully responding to challenges is an important part of male spirituality.

Ananias receives just such a challenge when God calls him to meet Saul. It is easy for us, knowing how the story turns out, to forget just how much God is asking of Ananias. This believer has heard "how much evil [Saul] has done to [God's] saints in Jerusalem" and how Saul has come to Damascus with authority from the chief priests to throw Christians into jail (vv. 13-14).

Yet Ananias' courage and trust in God allow him to be used by God to prepare Saul for the grand adventure God has in store for him: witnessing before Gentiles, kings, and the people of Israel—even though he also would suffer much for the sake of God's name.

—Matt Hamsher

Give me the courage and the strength today, Lord, to answer your call and accept your mission. May all that I do be for your glory and honor.

How have you been challenged to grow in your faith lately? How might you help others around you to have the courage to accept God's mission?

49. GOING OUT ON A LIMB

The voice said to [Peter] again, a second time, "What God has made clean, you must not call profane."—Acts 10:15

Scripture: Acts 10:1-35

I recently turned 50. As I look back, I see how much I've changed over the years. Things I took for granted are now very precious. Things I knew for certain now seem ambiguous. Things I never thought were true I have since come to embrace. Mostly, I've welcomed these gradual changes as part of growing up.

But I find the more abrupt changes to be harder to receive. This is where the story of Peter can help me. One day Peter has his world turned upside down by the Holy Spirit. Accepting Gentiles is not a trivial matter for this observant Jew. It touches the core of Peter's faith and demands a complete change of thought.

This story is really about trust. Peter walks out on a theological and cultural limb, following God's Spirit. Once there, he can never go back. It amazes me that it takes Peter only three tries to believe what the Spirit is saying. I'm not sure I'd be quite so trusting.

The older I get, the more lightly I hold my beliefs. They are no less important than they ever were. I just feel less need to protect them in their mint condition. I feel freer to let them rub up against new possibilities, even those that seem contradictory.

In the end, it comes down to trust—not in our beliefs themselves, but in the Spirit who calls us ever further out on the limb to new insights and commitments.

—Ron Adams

Lord, help me to let go of beliefs that keep me from growing closer to you. Free me to follow your Spirit, no matter where I'm led.

When has the Spirit called you to reexamine your beliefs? How will you respond the next time the Spirit calls?

50. FAITH FIGHTS AND FAITH FIRE

The disagreement became so sharp that [Paul and Barnabas] parted company.—Acts 15:39

Scripture: Acts 15:36-41

Paul and Barnabas differ "sharply" on how to get their missionary job done. These saints enter into passionate dialogue, get steamed up, perhaps clench fists, and then stomp apart to take separate, cooler paths. I've witnessed hot Christian moments, too—like church business meeting boil-ups, or pressure-cooker conflicts between pastor and antagonist. Brother-battles happen in a faith family.

To picture biblical heroes doing this is unsettling. But when we recognize that these faith founders are real people with actual issues and emotions, it helps us examine our own behaviors in our own fellowship fights. Becoming more self-aware, we see that where irreconcilable opinions are expressed, retreat may be the wisest and safest way to advance spiritually.

Failure to maintain fellowship doesn't always mean complete malfunction in God's mission for us as individuals or in our church community. Consider the successful ministry that Paul and Barnabas conduct after their break-up. Thankfully, Acts doesn't end there.

It's a fact that clashes between Christians burn believers and smoke up windows for seekers looking in. It's also true that God's Spirit heals and restores: Christians find forgiveness, churches experience growth. Believers can endure wounds. And honestly seeking souls can still come into this one house, where God mends them too.

The Taizé monastic community rules itself with these words: "Be consumed with zeal for the unity of the Body of Christ." That's a proper flame to keep ignited in our hearts when other flare-ups have, hopefully, cooled.

—Doug Schulz

Today as I sense hurts I've seen or caused in your body, Lord, please heal me or others as needed. And show me the path to true and enduring fellowship.

Try to measure the dimensions of the disagreements that you carry in your life right now. What path would God call you to take toward or away from your house-of-faith tensions?

51. GENTLE, PERSISTENT CRITIQUE

I opposed him to his face, because he stood self-condemned.
—Galatians 2:11

Scripture: Galatians 2:11-21

As a young adult I joined an intentional Christian community that was also a Mennonite congregation. More than a dozen people attended the congregation's worship and participated in its life yet did not feel led to commit to the membership requirement of the "common purse."

One year a man named Dave became a member but later objected to the rule that one had to submit to the common purse to be a member of the church. Most of us members disagreed with him, arguing that our practice was perfectly okay.

Unlike many others in history who simply left when their church didn't do what they thought was right, Dave persisted both as a member and as a gentle critic. He kept confronting our rule, saying that anyone should be able to join the church upon their confession of Jesus Christ as Lord.

Eventually we changed our practice and allowed people to join the congregation without joining the community of the common purse. Many took advantage of this. Dave was vindicated, but he never gloated or said, "I told you so."

Too many men either lack the courage to confront wrongdoing or react angrily and leave. When Christ's offer of grace and freedom is at stake, God calls us to follow Paul's example—to stand up for truth and to persist, lovingly, in promoting God's grace and shalom.

—Gordon Houser

Give me courage, Lord, to stand up for your offer of grace, and give me the grace to persist.

Have you confronted fellow Christians about principles of justice and grace? Have other Christians confronted you? What made for healthy (or unhealthy) outcomes?

52. HANG ON TO YOUR HERITAGE

I am reminded of your sincere faith, a faith that lived first in your grand-mother Lois and your mother Eunice and now, I am sure, lives in you.
—2 Timothy 1:5

Scripture: 2 Timothy 1:1-14

When my professor at seminary asked a visiting Egyptian Orthodox priest to say "a little bit about himself," I expected the usual five-minute bio about where he lived, the ages of his children, and the church he served. To my surprise he started by saying, "When Jesus was a small child, he fled to my country."

After some twenty minutes of passionately sharing how God had blessed the church in Egypt in the last 2,000 years, he told of the faith of his own ancestors from eight generations back.

I was startled at how much we miss in Western society when we introduce ourselves with information that only gets at a small slice of ourselves rather than the rich and godly heritage in which we are deeply grounded.

Paul mentions the "sincere" faith of Timothy's grandmother and mother, not only as a greeting but also as a teaching about the value of a godly heritage. Whether our Christian heritage is something that we can trace back through our biological family or through the saints of the church, Paul encourages us to know and to speak with confidence about the roots of the faith that lives within us.

—Allan Rudy-Froese

God, thank you for the strong roots of faith we share in the church family. Thank you for those in my life who have shown me the way to you.

Who are the saints (past or present) who serve as models for you? Would you dare to begin with them when someone asks you to "say a little bit about yourself"?

ACKNOWLEDGMENTS AND WRITER PROFILES

Wrestling with God began as an idea in the mind of Jim Gingerich and his colleagues in Mennonite Men, an organization that rallies men in Canada and the United States toward spiritual vitality and ministry. Jim, director of Mennonite Men, helped spearhead the development of the study series *Closer Than a Brother* (Faith & Life Resources) in the early 2000s. Mennonite Men covered many of the development costs for that series, as well as for the present volume. Thanks to Mennonite Men supporters for their interest and generosity.

In partnership with Faith & Life Resources, Jim appointed Gordon Houser and J. Lorne Peachey to develop an outline for *Wrestling with God*. FLR then assigned the writing to Mennonite writers on both sides of the border. Most of them are regular contributors to the Mennonite devotional magazine *Rejoice!* Many thanks to them for their creative work.

Our writers

Ron Adams is the lead pastor at East Chestnut Street Mennonite Church in Lancaster, Pennsylvania. He is married to Marilou, and is the father of two sons.

Leonard Beechy is a high school teacher in Goshen, Indiana, and a regular writer for the *Adult Bible Study* of Faith & Life Resources. He and his wife Sharon have two adult daughters.

Matt Hamsher is a doctoral student at Fuller Theological Seminary, Pasadena, California and a district elder for the Pacific Southwest Mennonite Conference. He and his wife Kristina share a home with their two daughters.

Gordon Houser is associate editor of *The Mennonite*, the denominational magazine of Mennonite Church USA. Gordon and his wife Jeanne live in Newton, Kansas, and are parents of two young adult children.

J. Lorne Peachey of Scottdale, Pennsylvania, is a volunteer editor for the Mennonite World Conference and former editor of *The Mennonite*. He helped outline this book in the same year his beloved wife Emily passed away. He has two grown children and one granddaughter.

Allan Rudy-Froese is a graduate student at the University of Toronto, with a background in pastoral work. He and his wife Marilyn live with their three children in Kitchener, Ontario.

Doug Schulz is a high school teacher from Vineland, Ontario, with experience in pastoral ministry, counseling, and writing. Doug is married to Annie, and they have three adult children.

Ervin Stutzman is dean at Eastern Mennonite Seminary, Harrisonburg, Virginia, former moderator of the Mennonite Church, and author of several books, including *Tobias of the Amish*. He and his wife Bonita have three adult children.

Philip Wiebe is former editor of *Rejoice!*, a columnist for the US Mennonite Brethren magazine *Christian Leader*, and an editor with the Oregon State Archives. He lives in Salem, Oregon, with his wife Kim and two children.